U0799508

冶金工业出版社

普通高等教育“十四五”规划教材

Business English—Communication Strategies for Career Development

商务英语—职业发展的沟通策略

孙成军　杨伟　徐建新　主编

Beijing
Metallurgical Industry Press
2025

Metallurgical Industry Press
39 Songzhuyuan North Alley, Dongcheng District, Beijing 100009, China

图书在版编目(CIP)数据

商务英语：职业发展的沟通策略 = Business English-Communication Strategies for Career Development：英文/孙成军，杨伟，徐建新主编. 北京：冶金工业出版社，2025.3. --（普通高等教育“十四五”规划教材）. --ISBN 978-7-5240-0047-1

Ⅰ. F7

中国国家版本馆 CIP 数据核字第 202413DH83 号

Business English—Communication Strategies for Career Development

出版发行	冶金工业出版社	**电　　话**	(010)64027926
地　　址	北京市东城区嵩祝院北巷 39 号	**邮　　编**	100009
网　　址	www.mip1953.com	**电子信箱**	service@mip1953.com

责任编辑　郭雅欣　美术编辑　吕欣童　版式设计　郑小利
责任校对　梁江凤　责任印制　禹　蕊
北京建宏印刷有限公司印刷
2025 年 3 月第 1 版，2025 年 3 月第 1 次印刷
787mm×1092mm　1/16；8.5 印张；204 千字；123 页
定价 36.00 元

投稿电话　(010)64027932　投稿信箱　tougao@cnmip.com.cn
营销中心电话　(010)64044283
冶金工业出版社天猫旗舰店　yjgycbs.tmall.com
（本书如有印装质量问题，本社营销中心负责退换）

Preface

Business English plays an important role in the globalized business environment. It is not only a bridge for communication in international trade and multinational corporations but also an essential tool for acquiring the latest business information, expanding business networks, and enhancing professional competitiveness. Mastering Business English can help individuals and enterprises participate more effectively in international market exchanges, improve communication efficiency, promote business cooperation, and ultimately achieve commercial success.

The original intention of writing this book is to help readers who wish to improve their English communication skills in a business environment. Business communication is not just simple verbal transmission; it involves various complex situations. For example, how to start a conversation at a party or wedding, how to make suggestions in a work meeting, how to answer questions in a job interview, etc. To systematically present these skills, the content of this book is divided into 11 thematic units, each providing practical communication strategies and advice for specific situations. At the same time, it also focuses on how to establish good relationships with managers, colleagues, and employees—for instance, how to earn a manager's trust, how to communicate with difficult colleagues, and how to manage and support employees.

The materials and content of each unit in this book are carefully designed. Unit 1 provides a detailed introduction to the differences between formal and informal language, enabling readers to choose appropriate expressions according to different occasions. Units 2 to 11 explore how to communicate effectively in a business environment through a series of situational dialogues. In addition, this book not only offers comprehensive methodological guidance but also includes a large number of examples, dialogues, and exercises to help readers become familiar with the business environment, learn quickly, and enhance their practical application skills.

Due to the limitations of the authors' abilities, any shortcomings in the book are earnestly welcomed for correction and assistance from readers.

Authors

May 2024

Contents

Unit 1　Formal and informal language

In communication, the use of formal and informal language varies depending on different occasions and audiences. To maintain professionalism or communicate with diverse audiences, it's essential to understand when and how to use these two language styles. This unit will provide a comprehensive overview of scenarios, techniques, and examples of formal and informal language, assisting everyone in using English appropriately and effectively in various contexts. Let's delve deep and master these two distinct styles to prepare for both daily conversations and professional situations.

在交流中，正式语言和非正式语言的使用根据不同的场合和对象而变化。为了保持专业度或与不同的受众沟通，我们需要了解何时及如何使用这两种语言风格。本单元将详细介绍正式语言和非正式语言的情境、使用技巧和示例，帮助您更好地在各种场合下使用英语，确保有效并恰当地传达信息。让我们深入了解并掌握这两种不同的语言风格，为日常沟通和专业场合做好准备。

1.1　Scenarios for formal and informal language

Formal scenarios　正式情境	**Informal scenarios　非正式情境**
When you are communicating with someone that you don't know very well 当你与不太熟悉的人交流时	Situations that are relaxed and that involve people that you know well or know each other well 轻松的情境，涉及你熟悉的人或彼此熟悉的人
Business emails　商务电子邮件	Personal emails　个人电子邮件
Academic writing/articles　学术写作/论文	Everyday conversations　日常对话
Presentations　演讲文稿	Social media　社交媒体
Reports　报告	Advertising　广告
Public tenders　公开招标	Spontaneous speech　即兴演讲
Official documents　官方文件	Text messages　文字信息

Talking to superiors 与上级交谈	Talking to peers 与同龄人交谈
Legal documents 法律文件	Meeting minutes 会议记录
Public speaking (speeches, lectures, etc.) 公开演讲(演说,讲座等)	Networking or socializing with clients 与客户建立关系或进行社交
Job interviews 工作面试	Team meetings 团队会议

1.2 Tips on how to use formal and informal language

Formal 正式	**Informal 非正式**
No contractions 无缩略词	Contractions 缩略词
No phrasal verbs 无短语动词	Phrasal verbs 短语动词
No idioms 无俚语	Idioms 俚语
No abbreviations 无缩写	Abbreviations 缩写
Passive voice 被动语态	Active voice 主动语态
No imperatives 无祈使句	Imperatives 祈使句
No exclamation marks 无感叹号	Exclamation marks 感叹号
No emojis 无表情符号	Emojis 表情符号
Professional verbs 专业动词	General verbs 一般动词
No Chinglish 无中式英语	Chinglish 中式英语

1.3 Examples of formal and informal language

1.3.1 Contractions

(1) 由于资金限制,新技术无法引入。

Formal: The new technology **cannot** be introduced due to funding restrictions.

Informal: The new technology **can't** be introduced due to funding restrictions.

(2) 我们立即采取行动非常重要。

Formal: **It is** important that we act immediately.

Informal: **It's** important that we act immediately.

(3) 研究项目明天不会开始。

Formal: The research project **will not** start tomorrow.

Informal: The research project **won't** start tomorrow.

1.3.2 Phrasal verbs

(1) 董事会将调查此事。

Formal: The board will **investigate** the matter.

Informal: The board will **look into** the matter.

(2) 由于停电，机器出现了故障。

Formal: The machine **malfunctioned** due to a power outage.

Informal: The machine **broke down** due to a power outage.

(3) 会议已经推迟到下周。

Formal: The meeting has been **postponed** until next week.

Informal: The meeting has been **put off** until next week.

1.3.3 Idioms

(1) 恐怕我们必须推迟我们的会议。

Formal: I am afraid we have to **postpone** our meeting.

Informal: I'm afraid we have to **rain check** our meeting.

(2) 讲师希望学生在论文中使用正确的语法和标点符号。

Formal: Lecturers **expect** students to use correct grammar and punctuation in essays.

Informal: Lecturers **count on** students to use correct grammar and punctuation in essays.

(3) 雨正下得很大。

Formal: It is raining **very heavily**.

Informal: It is raining **cats and dogs**.

1.3.4 Abbreviations

(1) 请尽快把项目更新发给我，以便我们为下周的会议做准备。

Formal: Please send me the project updates **as soon as possible** so we can prepare for the meeting next week.

Informal: Please send me the project updates **ASAP** so we can prepare for the meeting next week.

(2) 顺便说一下，明天别忘了带伞，因为天气预报预测会下雨。

Formal: **By the way**, do not forget to bring your umbrella tomorrow as the weather forecast predicts rain.

Informal: **BTW**, don't forget to bring your umbrella tomorrow as the weather forecast predicts rain.

(3) 公司发起了一场新的广告活动以推广其最新产品。

Formal: The company launched a new **advertisement** campaign to promote its latest product.

Informal：The company launched a new **ad** campaign to promote its latest product.

1.3.5 Voices

（1）我填写了申请表格。

Formal：The application form **was completed** by me.（被动语态）

Informal：I **completed** the application form.（主动语态）

（2）这项研究发现体育锻炼和心理健康之间存在显著的相关性。

Formal：A significant correlation between physical exercise and mental health **was found** in the study.（被动语态）

Informal：The study **found** a significant correlation between physical exercise and mental health.（主动语态）

（3）文献综述突出了几个重要的发现。

Formal：Several significant findings **are highlighted** in the literature review.（被动语态）

Informal：The literature review **highlights** several significant findings.（主动语态）

1.3.6 Imperatives

（1）完成这个表格。

Formal：The form is to **be completed at your earliest convenience**.

Informal：**Complete** the form.

（2）关上门。

Formal：**It would be most appreciated** if the door were closed.

Informal：**Close** the door.

（3）吃掉你的蔬菜。

Formal：**It would be healthy to consume** your vegetables.

Informal：**Eat** your vegetables.

1.3.7 Exclamation marks

（1）你的申请已经被批准了。

Formal：I am pleased to inform you that your application has been approved.

Informal：Hey，great news！Your application has been approved！

（2）提交的截止日期快到了，请确保你的文件已经完成并按时发送。

Formal：The deadline for submission is approaching，so please ensure that your documents are completed and sent in a timely manner.

Informal：Just a heads up！The deadline is coming up，so make sure you finish your documents and send them on time！

（3）对于包裹延迟送达而给你带来的不便，我深感抱歉。

Formal：I apologize for the inconvenience caused by the delay in delivery of your package.

Informal：Sorry about the delay in delivery of your package！

1.3.8 Emojis

(1) 我期待着参加今晚的社交活动。

Formal: I am looking forward to attending the social event this evening.

Informal: I'm so excited for the party tonight! 

(2) 你好，你愿意晚些时候和我一起吃比萨吗?

Formal: Hello, would you like to join me for a meal consisting of pizza at a later time?

Informal: Hey, wanna grab some pizza later? 

(3) 我渴望能够亲自见到你。

Formal: I am eager to meet you in person.

Informal: Can't wait to see you! 

1.3.9 Lexical verbs

(1) 我收到了你的电子邮件。

Formal: I **received** your email. (专业动词)

Informal: I **got** your email. (一般动词)

(2) 为了确保项目的成功，我们保留经验丰富的员工是至关重要的。

Formal: To ensure the project's success, it's crucial that we **retain** our experienced staff members. (专业动词)

Informal: To ensure the project's success, it's crucial that we **keep** our experienced staff members. (一般动词)

(3) 我想学习更多关于人工智能的知识以提升我的技能。

Formal: I **desire** to learn more about artificial intelligence to improve my skills. (专业动词)

Informal: I **want** to learn more about artificial intelligence to improve my skills. (一般动词)

1.3.10 Chinglish

(1) 这个不好，真的很不舒服。

Formal: This one **is not** good, **and it is really** uncomfortable.

Informal: This one **no** good, **very no** comfortable.

(2) 我恳求你听从我的建议，你明天必须早点到学校。

Formal: I **implore you to heed my advice**, and it is imperative that you **arrive at school at an earlier time** tomorrow.

Informal: You **listen me**, tomorrow you **early come school**.

(3) 他昨天的缺席让我感到非常沮丧。

Formal: His **absence yesterday induced a significant amount of frustration in me**.

Informal: He **yesterday didn't come**, **made me angry**.

1.4 Example of application

Formal

Dear Mr. Thompson,

Per our recent communication, the annual report has been meticulously reviewed and certain discrepancies have been identified. Said discrepancies were uncovered by our dedicated finance team. The report, which was compiled by the team, indicates that some figures require further clarification. To ensure complete accuracy, it is requested that a meeting be scheduled at your earliest convenience. A comprehensive understanding of the figures will enable us to present the report confidently at the upcoming board meeting. Your assistance in this matter would be greatly appreciated.

Awaiting your prompt response.

Sincerely, Jane Smith

Informal

Hey Tom,

Got your mail about the annual report, and dude, there are some funky numbers in there. Our finance peeps did a deep dive and found some stuff that doesn't quite add up. We gotta get together and sort this out ASAP! I mean, we need to have this on point before the big meeting, right? Let's catch up and hammer this out. Drop me a line when you're free, and we'll set something up. And BTW, don't stress too much. We'll fix this!

Catch ya later,

Jane

Exercises

1-1 Write a short paragraph explaining a situation where formal language would be appropriate and another where informal language would be better.

1-2 Translate the following Chinglish sentences into standard English.

(1) No can do.

(2) This no my car.

(3) You look me, I look you.

(4) People mountain people sea.

(5) You have a nose very big.

(6) Eat the medicine.

(7) He can speak English very good.

(8) I very like this movie.

1-3 Read through the two letters below, and identify the differences between them based on formal and informal language.

Formal	Informal
Dear Sir/Madam,	Hello!
I am writing to complain about an incident that occurred in your restaurant at around 7 pm last Friday.	Let me tell you what happened when I visited your restaurant last week.
While my family and I were enjoying our meal, we overheard staff members arguing in the restaurant. This type of behavior is extremely unprofessional and particularly distressing for my kids to have to hear.	I'm a regular there. I came to the restaurant with my family. The food was on point but then we heard your staff shouting really loudly!
My family and I have been regular customers at your restaurant for years, and we hope that we can continue to enjoy your service.	This put me off my food! I mean c'mon is that professional? My child got upset. I was very angry.
I trust that you will investigate this matter and take the necessary actions required to ensure customer satisfaction.	You need to look into this matter please. Do what is needed to make sure your customers are happy!
I look forward to hearing from you.	Please reply ASAP.

1-4 Read the four choices marked A, B, C and D, and decide which is the best answer to each question.

(1) Formal language is used in ____.

A. all situations

B. professional situations

C. unprofessional situations

D. informal social gatherings

(2) Informal language is used in ____.

A. all situations

B. professional situations

C. unprofessional situations

D. casual or social situations

(3) What is a contraction? ____.

A. The full version of a word

B. A phrasal verb

C. A shortened version of a word

D. A complex sentence

(4) "Point out" is an example of a/an ____.

A. abbreviation

B. acronym

C. phrasal verb

D. contraction

(5) "Break a leg" is an example of a ____.

A. phrasal verb

B. contraction

C. idiom

D. acronym

(6) Which sentence uses formal language? ____

A. I got you.

B. I understand what you are saying.

C. Gotcha!

D. I reckon so.

(7) Which sentence uses informal language? ____

A. I am unable to attend the meeting scheduled for tomorrow due to a prior engagement.

B. FYI, the grocery store has a sale on all produce items this weekend.

C. In light of recent developments, it has become imperative for us to reconsider our strategies.

D. We are currently in the process of reviewing our business model.

(8) Which sentence does not use Chinglish ____

A. Do you like to drink porridge?

B. His classmate made exercise yesterday.

C. I hope I can go home early.

D. This one how much money?

(9) In formal language sentences, there cannot be imperatives, exclamation marks, or emojis. Is this statement correct? ____

A. Yes.

B. No.

C. Partially correct.

D. It depends on the context.

Unit 2　Email communication

In this digital era, email has become an indispensable communication tool in our daily lives and work. This unit provides a detailed breakdown of the various components of an email. From choosing the appropriate salutations to drafting a clear and structured email body, from selecting the right closing remarks to designing a signature block, and understanding when to capitalize as well as how to make effective use of spacing and empty lines, we will explain each aspect step by step. Let's learn together to make your email communication more professional and efficient.

在这个数字化时代，电子邮件已成为我们日常生活和工作中不可或缺的沟通工具。本单元为你详细解读电子邮件的各个组成部分。从如何选择恰当的称呼，到撰写条理清晰的邮件正文，从结束语的选择到签名档的设计，再到何时应使用大写、如何合理使用间距与空行，本单元都会逐一讲解。让我们共同学习，使你的邮件沟通更加专业、高效。

2.1　Parts of an email

电子邮件的组成如图 2-1 所示。

	To：Mr. Smith@ BusinessEnglish. com
Subject　主题	Subject：Project Status and Next Steps
Salutation　问候语	Dear Mr. Smith,
Body　正文	I hope this finds you well. I wanted to update you on our project status. We've completed Task A and B is nearing completion. Task C is now underway. We're on track with our timeline, aiming to start Task D in the next quarter. If you have any questions or would like to discuss further, please let me know. I'm happy to schedule a meeting at your earliest convenience.
Closing　结束语	Best Regards,
Signature　签名	Mike Turner
Signature block (optional) 签名档（可选）	(212) 555-1234 Mike. Turner@ Hi-Tech. com

图 2-1　电子邮件的组成

2.2 Email salutations

Formal—Use a colon (:)
Dear Hiring Manager:
Dear Professor Turner:
Dear Board of Directors:
(1) Job applications 求职
(2) Leaders in your company, school or community 公司、学校或社区的领导
(3) Other people in higher positions 其他职位更高的人

Neutral—Use a comma (,)
Dear Mom and Dad,
Dear Mike,
(1) Friends and family 朋友和家人
(2) People you see daily or often 你每天或经常见到的人
(3) Teachers or professors (depending on culture and relationship) 老师或教授（根据当地文化和你们的关系）

Informal—Use Hello/Hi+Name, or Hi/Hey,
Hello/Hi Mike,
Hi/Hey,
(1) close friends 亲密的朋友
(2) close colleagues 亲密的同事
(3) close peers 亲密的同龄人

2.3 Email body

2.3.1 Introducing topic

(1) I'm writing regarding **the issues we've been having with our database system.**
我写这封信是关于**我们的数据库系统一直存在的问题**。
(2) I wanted to follow up on **our meeting last week and confirm our plans for this month.**
我想跟进**上周的会议，并确认本月的计划**。
(3) I would like to ask about **the new budget and whether this will affect our department.**
我想问一下**新的预算以及这是否会影响我们部门**。
(4) Do you know **when the database issues will be fixed**?
你知道**数据库的问题什么时候能修复吗**？
(5) Let's confirm **our plans for this month.**
让我们确认**这个月的计划**。

(6) How will **the new budget** affect **our department**?
新的预算会如何影响**我们部门**？

(7) I'm concerned about **the number of sick days staff have been taking recently**.
我对**最近员工请病假的天数**较为关切。

(8) I need to bring something to your attention: **using outdated software puts us at risk of malware infections and data loss**.
我需要提醒你一件事：**使用过时的软件会使我们面临恶意软件感染和数据丢失的风险**。

2.3.2 Adding details to your topic

(1) I'm writing regarding issues we've been having with our database.
我写这封信是关于我们的数据库一直存在的问题。

Both clients and staff have been experiencing severe problems for several days now. We are unable to update records or access information on customer interaction. This is costing us large amounts of money, both in time spent trying to fix the problem, and in lost sales.
这几天来，客户和员工都遇到了严重的问题。我们无法更新记录或获取客户的互动信息。这让我们损失了大量的金钱，包括花费在解决问题上的时间和销售损失。

(2) I'm concerned about the number of sick days staff have been taking recently.
我对最近员工请病假天数较为关切。

Staff in the IT department have taken a total of 44 sick days so far this month, compared to a total of 23 for last month, and just 18 for the previous month. This is affecting productivity, and also placing a lot of stress on employees who do come to work.
本月到目前为止，IT 部门的员工总共请了 44 天病假，上个月总共请了 23 天病假，上上个月只有 18 天。这影响了部门产出，也给到岗员工带来了很大的压力。

2.3.3 Changing topic (optional)

(1) There's one more thing I'd like to discuss with you.
还有一件事我想和你讨论一下。

(2) Regarding...
关于……

(3) I'd also like to ask you about...
我还想问你关于……

(4) There's one more thing I'd like to discuss with you. It seems like the number of customer complaints has been increasing for three months...
还有一件事我想和你讨论一下。好像三个月来客户投诉的数量一直在增加……

2.3.4 Adding a call-to-action to explain what you need the other person to do

(1) Please **arrange a meeting of all department heads** by tomorrow at the latest.
请最迟在明天之前**安排一场所有部门主管参加的会议**。

(2) As a matter of urgency, you need to **contact all the clients who may have been affected**

by this data breach.

紧急情况下，你需要**联系所有可能受到此次数据泄露影响的客户**。

(3) Could you please **talk to Mike in the HR department and clarify our options on this**?

你能不能和人力资源部的迈克谈谈，澄清一下我们在这方面的选择？

(4) I would like you to **design a poster to inform staff about the new policies.**

我想请你设计一张海报，以告知员工新政策。

(5) I suggest that you **contact all clients who may have been affected by the data breach.**

我建议你**联系所有可能受到数据泄露影响的客户**。

(6) Can I ask you to **design a poster to inform staff about the new policies**?

我能请你设计一张海报，以告知员工新政策吗？

2.3.5 If you don't need a response from the other person (optional)

(1) This is just to keep you updated.

本邮件只是为了让你了解最新情况。

(2) This doesn't require any immediate response, but please keep an eye on the situation.

本邮件不需要立即回应，但请密切关注事态发展。

Example

Dear Mike,

Part 1	I need to bring something to your attention: many staff are using very weak passwords on their laptops and for database access.
Part 2	Our work depends on keeping our clients' personal financial information safe. If we lose our clients' trust on this issue, it will not be easy to recover. I trust that you can see that it is better to take action now, rather than after something goes wrong.
Part 3	I suggest we make a rule that passwords must be a specific length, and that staff must change their passwords at least once a month. Please let me know what you think about this.

Regards,

Julia

2.4 Email closings

Formal 正式	Informal 非正式	More personal 更个人化	Innovative 创新性的
Kind regards,	Cheers,	See you soon,	Be well,

Sincerely,	Best,	All the best,	Dream big,
Respectfully,	Take care,	Keep in touch,	Stay gold,
Yours faithfully,	Stay awesome,	Wishing you well,	Stay curious,
With gratitude,	Talk soon,	Peace and love,	Onward and upward,
With appreciation,	Catch you later,	Miss you,	To infinity and beyond,

2. 5 Signature block

Example 1

Mike Turner
Mike. Turner@ Hi-Tech. com
www. Hi-Tech. com

Example 2

Mike Turner
(212) 555-1234
Project Manager, Hi-Tech Company
2010 Main St. , Winnipeg, MB, R2V 2A5

2. 6 What to capitalize

Capitalize the following words in subject:
邮件主题中下列单词大写:
First word 第一个词
Last word 最后一个词
Important words 重要词
Capitalize the first word and all nouns in salutations
称呼中的第一个词和所有名词的首字母都要大写
Capitalize the first word in closings
结束语的第一个单词首字母大写

To: mr. Smith@ BusinessEnglish. com
Subject: **Project Status** and **Next Steps**

Dear Mr. Smith,
I hope this finds you well. I wanted to update you on our project status.
We've completed Task A and B is nearing completion. Task C is now underway. We're on track with our timeline, aiming to start Task D in the next quarter.
If you have any questions or would like to discuss further, please let me know. I'm happy to schedule a meeting at your earliest convenience.
Best regards,
Mike Turner
(212) 555-1234
Mike. Turner@ Hi-Tech. com

2.7 What are important words

Important words

Nouns: people: teacher, parent, boy, etc.
places: school, library, city, etc.
things: book, idea, homework, etc.

Verbs: run, ask, speak, etc.

Adjectives: difficult, charming, sunny, etc.

Adverbs: not, always, immediately, etc.

Not important words

Articles: a, an, the.

Conjunctions: and, but, or, etc.

Prepositions: in, on, of, etc.

2.8 Spacing and empty lines

In an email, spacing usually refers to the gaps between lines or paragraphs. It can be adjusted to single spacing, 1.5 spacing, double spacing, etc., depending on the email client or software you are using.

在电子邮件中，间距通常指的是行与行或段落之间的空隙。根据你使用的电子邮件客户端或软件，可以调整为单倍行距、1.5 倍行距、双倍行距等。

Empty lines are lines without any text or content. They are often used to separate paragraphs, to differentiate between the opening and the body of the email, or to create a break before a conclusion or signature.

空行是指没有任何文本或内容的行。它们通常用于分隔段落，区分电子邮件的开头和正文，或者在结论或签名之前制造一个停顿。

电子邮件的间距和空行案例如图 2-2 所示。

> To: mr. Smith@ BusinessEnglish. com
> Subject: Project Status and Next Steps
> Dear Mr. Smith,
> ——→*Empty line after salutation* 问候语后空行
> I hope this finds you well. I wanted to update you on our project status.
> ——→*Empty line between paragraphs* 段落间空行
> We've completed Task A and B is nearing completion. Task C is now underway. We're on track with our timeline, aiming to start Task D in the next quarter.
> ——→*Empty line between paragraphs* 段落间空行

If you have any questions or would like to discuss further, please let me know. I'm happy to schedule a meeting at your earliest convenience.
——→*Empty line before closing* 结束语前空行
Best Regards,
——→ *Empty line after closing* 结束语后空行
Mike Turner
(212) 555-1234 ——→*No empty line after signature* 签名后无空行
Mike. Turner@ Hi-Tech. com

图 2-2 电子邮件的间距和空行

Exercises

2-1 Below is a sample email. Read it carefully and identify the following parts: salutation, body, closing and signature block.

Subject: Meeting Schedule
Dear Team,

I hope this email finds you well. I'd like to propose a meeting for next Tuesday at 3 pm to discuss our next project. Please let me know if this time works for you.

Best regards,

Mike Turner
Project Manager
Mike. Turner@ example. com
+123-456-7890

2-2 Below is an email with formatting errors. Correct the email to ensure proper capitalization, spacing, and empty lines.

Subject: Update needed

hello team,

there are some updates in our project. I hope everyone will be available for the meeting on Friday at 2 pm. See you all there.

Thanks,
mike turner.
Product Manager.
Mike. Turner@ example. com.

2-3 Create your own professional email signature block. Remember to include your full name, position or role, and contact information.

2-4 Compose a business email based on the following scenario: You are the manager at a tech company and you need to inform your team about a change in the project deadline. Make sure to include all parts of an email and follow proper email etiquette.

Unit 3 How to start a conversation

Whether in daily life or in a professional environment, establishing contact and initiating a conversation with others is an essential skill. Casual chats with friends, reunions with friends you haven't seen in a long time, interactions with colleagues, or building new relationships in various social events such as parties, weddings, or work conferences all require different approaches to start. Moreover, initiating a conversation with a stranger requires both tact and courage. This unit will provide you with methods and techniques for starting conversations in various situations, helping you connect with others with greater confidence.

无论是在日常生活中还是在职场环境中，与他人建立联系和开启对话都是非常重要的技能。与朋友轻松聊天、与长时间未见的朋友重逢、与同事交往，或是在各种社交场合，如派对、婚礼、工作会议上与他人建立新的关系，都需要不同的开场方式。此外，与陌生人开启对话更需要技巧与勇气。本单元将为你提供各种场合下开启对话的方法与技巧，帮助你更自信地与他人建立联系。

3.1 With friends

(1) A：What's up?

B：Not much, just been keeping busy with work. How about you? What's new?

A：最近怎么样？

B：没什么特别的，就是一直忙于工作。你呢？有什么新鲜事吗？

(2) A：What's new?

B：Well, I've recently started a new project at work which is pretty exciting! What's new with you?

A：有什么新鲜事吗？

B：嗯，我最近在工作中开始了一个新的项目，非常令人兴奋！你呢？有什么新鲜事吗？

(3) A：How's it going?

B：Great/Good/Not so good.

A：最近过得怎么样？

B：很好/好/不太好。

(4) A：Hi Julia! How's your week been so far?

B：Hi Mike! It's been good, quite busy. How about you? How are things going on your end?

A：嗨，茱莉亚！你这周过得怎么样？

B：嗨，迈克！还不错，挺忙的。你呢？你那边情况如何？

3.2 With friends you haven't seen in a long time

(1) A：Hi Julia! How have you been?

B：Hi! It's so great to see you. I've been really well, thanks for asking. Life's kept me pretty busy. How about you? How have you been doing?

A：嗨，茱莉亚！你近来怎么样？

B：嗨！很高兴见到你。我过得很好，感谢你的询问。最近我忙得不可开交。你呢？你近来怎么样？

(2) A：Long time no see!

B：Indeed! It's been ages. It's so great to catch up with you. How have you been?

A：好久不见！

B：的确是！已经好久了。能跟你聊聊真好。你近来怎么样？

(3) A：So, what have you been up to lately?

B：Oh, quite a lot! I've taken on some exciting new projects at work, started learning to play the piano, and have been trying out some new hiking trails in the area. How about you? What have you been up to?

A：那么，你最近在忙些什么？

B：哦，有很多事情！我在工作中接手了一些令人兴奋的新项目，开始学习弹钢琴，并尝试了本地一些新的徒步路线。你呢？你最近在忙些什么？

(4) A：How's your family?

B：My family is doing well, thank you. We've had our ups and downs, as always, but overall, we're in good spirits. How about yours? It's been such a long time since we last talked.

A：你的家人好吗？

B：我的家人都很好，谢谢。像往常一样，我们经历了起起伏伏，但总的来说，我们的精神状态很好。自从我们上次交谈以后已经过了很久了。

(5) A：Are you still working at ABC company?

B：No, actually, I left ABC company about a year ago. I'm now working with XYZ Corp., and it's a refreshing change. How about you? What's new on your end?

A：你还在 ABC 公司工作吗？

B：不，其实我大约一年前离开了 ABC 公司。我现在在 XYZ 公司工作，这是一个令人耳目一新的改变。你呢？你那边有什么新鲜事吗？

3.3 With colleagues

(1) A：Julia, I know you're a big fan of cooking. I've been trying to improve my skills in the kitchen lately. Do you have any beginner-friendly recipes or tips to share?

B：Of course! I'd be happy to share some of my favorite recipes and cooking tips with you.

A：茱莉亚，我知道你热衷烹饪。我最近一直在努力提高我的厨艺。你有没有适合初学者的食谱或烹饪技巧可以分享？

B：当然！我很乐意与你分享我最喜欢的食谱和烹饪技巧。

(2) A：Hi, Julia. How are you doing?

B：I'm doing well, thank you. How about you?

A：嗨，茱莉亚。你最近怎么样？

B：我很好，谢谢你。你呢？

(3) A：We're sure having a busy/slow day today.

B：Absolutely, it's non-stop action today! But it feels good to be productive. How are you managing?

A：我们今天真的很忙。

B：绝对地，今天忙得停不下来！但是感觉很有成效。你做得如何？

(4) A：Have you heard the news about the recent earthquake in Japan?

B：Yes, I did. It's quite heartbreaking. I hope the rescue and relief operations are going smoothly.

A：你听说最近日本发生地震的新闻了吗？

B：是的，我听说了。真是令人心痛。我希望救援和救灾行动能够顺利进行。

(5) A：Have you got any plans for the weekend?

B：Yes, I'm planning to visit a local art exhibition and maybe do a little bit of hiking if the weather's good. How about you? Any plans?

A：周末有什么计划吗？

B：有，我打算去参观一个当地的艺术展览，如果天气好的话，可能会去轻装徒步。你呢？有什么计划吗？

(6) A：How was your weekend?

B：It was really lovely, thank you! I visited the art exhibition as planned and managed to go hiking as well. The weather was perfect. How was yours?

A：你的周末过得怎么样？

B：真的非常愉快，谢谢你！我按计划参观了艺术展览，也去徒步了。天气非常好。你的周末过得怎样？

3.4 At a party/wedding

(1) A: I don't think we've met—I'm Mike.

B: Nice to meet you, Mike. I'm Julia. Are you a friend of the hosts, or how did you end up at this party/wedding?

A: 我想这是我们初次见面——我是迈克。

B: 很高兴认识你，迈克。我是茱莉亚。你是主人的朋友吗，或者你是怎么决定来参加这个派对/婚礼的?

(2) A: Are you from New York?

B: Oh, no, I'm actually from Los Angeles. How about you? Are you from New York?

A: 你来自纽约吗?

B: 哦，不，实际上我来自洛杉矶。你呢?你来自纽约吗?

(3) A: So, how do you know Julia?

B: Julia is my cousin! We've known each other since we were kids. It's great to see her at this party/wedding. How about you? How do you know Julia?

A: 那么，你是怎么认识茱莉亚的?

B: 茱莉亚是我的表亲!我们从小就认识。在这个派对/婚礼上看到她真好。你呢?你是怎么认识茱莉亚的?

(4) A: Have you tried the chocolate cake? It's delicious!

B: Oh, not yet, but I've heard great things about it! I'll definitely give it a try. Thanks for the recommendation!

A: 你试过巧克力蛋糕吗?它非常美味!

B: 哦，还没有，但我听说它很好吃!我肯定会去试试的。谢谢你的推荐!

3.5 At a conference/work event

(1) A: I don't think we've met—I'm Mike.

B: Hi Mike, nice to meet you! I'm Julia. Are you enjoying the conference/work event so far?

A: 我想这是我们初次见面——我是迈克。

B: 嗨，迈克，很高兴认识你!我是茱莉亚。你觉得这个会议/工作活动如何?

(2) A: So, where are you from?

B: I'm originally from Seattle, but currently, I live in San Francisco. How about you? Where are you from?

A: 那么，你来自哪里?

B: 我是西雅图人，但现在住在旧金山。你呢?你来自哪里?

(3) A：What did you think of the speaker?

B：Oh, I found the speaker very engaging and informative. He had some excellent insights on the topic. What about you? Did you enjoy the presentation?

A：你觉得演讲者怎么样？

B：哦，我觉得演讲者非常有趣，演讲内容丰富。他对这个主题有一些极好的见解。你呢？你喜欢这个演讲吗？

(4) A：That was an excellent workshop—I learned a lot. How about you?

B：I completely agree! It was a valuable workshop, and I also learned a great deal. The presenter was fantastic. I'm glad I attended. Is there any other session you're looking forward to during this event?

A：这次的研讨会太棒了——我学到了很多。你呢？

B：我完全同意！这是一场有价值的研讨会，我也学到了很多。主讲人非常出色。我很高兴参加了这次研讨会。在这个活动中，你还期待其他什么会议吗？

3.6 With someone you were just introduced to

(1) A：Nice to meet you!

B：Nice to meet you too! How are you enjoying the event/gathering so far?

A：很高兴见到你！

B：也很高兴见到你！到目前为止，你觉得这个活动/聚会如何？

(2) A：How do you two know each other?

B：Oh, we actually just met a little while ago! It's been great getting to know each other. How about you? Have you known each other for a while?

A：你们俩是怎么认识的？

B：哦，我们其实刚刚才认识不久！很高兴能够结识对方。你呢？你们认识很久了吗？

(3) A：So, what do you do for a living?

B：I work as a marketing manager for a software company. It's an exciting role, and I enjoy the challenges it brings. How about you? What do you do?

A：你的工作是什么？

B：我在一家软件公司担任市场经理。这是一个令人振奋的角色，我喜欢它带来的挑战。你呢？你做什么工作？

(4) A：What are you studying?

B：I'm currently studying computer science at university. It's a fascinating field, and I'm really enjoying it so far. How about you?

A：你在学什么？

B：我目前在大学学习计算机科学。这是一个非常吸引人的领域，到目前为止我非常享受。你呢？

(5) A：How long have you been doing yoga?

B：I started practicing yoga about 3 years ago, and it has been so beneficial for my well-being. How about you? Do you have any hobbies or interests that you've been passionate about for a long time?

A：你练习瑜伽有多久了？

B：我大约 3 年前开始练习瑜伽，这对我的身心健康非常有益。你呢？你有什么长期热衷的爱好或兴趣吗？

3.7 With someone you meet outside

(1) A：It's a beautiful day, isn't it?

B：Yes, it really is! The weather couldn't be better. It's so refreshing to be outside on such a lovely day. How are you enjoying the weather?

A：今天天气很好，不是吗？

B：是的，确实如此！天气再好不过了。在如此美好的一天外出真是令人振奋。你喜欢这个天气吗？

(2) A：It looks like it's going to rain.

B：Oh, you're right. It does seem like the clouds are getting darker. I hope it doesn't rain too heavily, I didn't bring an umbrella.

A：看起来好像要下雨了。

B：哦，你说得对。看起来云层的颜色似乎越来越暗。希望雨不会下太大，我没有带伞。

(3) A：Can you believe all this rain we've been having?

B：Absolutely! It feels like it's been raining forever! The weather has been quite unpredictable lately. I'm hoping for some sunny days soon. How have you been coping with all the rain?

A：你能相信我们最近的雨量吗？

B：当然！感觉好像一直在下雨！最近的天气真的很难预测。我希望很快就能有阳光明媚的日子。你如何应对这么多的雨？

(4) A：Sure is a cold one today!

B：Oh, absolutely! It's freezing out here. I should have brought a heavier coat. How are you managing with the cold weather?

A：今天真是冷啊！

B：哦，绝对的！这里真的很冷。我应该带一件更厚的外套。你是如何应对这个冷天气的？

(5) A：Just look at those flowers. They're amazing, aren't they?

B：Oh, they really are stunning! I love how vibrant and colorful they are. It's such a lovely sight. Do you have a favorite type of flower?

A：看看那些花。它们很美，不是吗？

B：哦，它们真的很漂亮！我喜欢它们的鲜艳和多彩。这是一道如此美丽的风景。你有最喜欢的花吗？

(6) A：Your dog is so cute! What's his name?

B：Thank you! His name is Mike. Do you have any pets of your own?

A：你的狗真可爱！它叫什么名字？

B：谢谢你！它的名字是迈克。你有宠物吗？

3.8 With a stranger (in other contexts)

3.8.1 At a sports game

(1) A：Wow, that was a great play! So, who's your favorite player?

B：Oh, I'm a big fan of Mike, number 24. His speed and agility never fail to amaze me. How about you?

A：哇，那是一场很棒的比赛！那么，你最喜欢的球员是谁？

B：哦，我是 24 号迈克的超级粉丝。他的速度和敏捷总是让我吃惊。你呢？

(2) A：The game is so intense! Did you expect Team A to be leading by this much?

B：Honestly, no! I always thought Team B had a stronger defense. It's full of surprises. Who are you rooting for?

A：这场比赛太激烈了！你预料到 A 队会领先这么多吗？

B：老实说，没有！我一直认为 B 队的防守更强。真是充满了惊喜。你支持哪一队？

3.8.2 At a café

(1) A：Boy, I do need a coffee!

B：I hear you on that! The lattes here are usually really good. Have you tried one before?

A：天啊，我需要一杯咖啡！

B：我明白你的意思！这里的拿铁通常都很好喝。你以前喝过吗？

(2) A：The pastries here look so tempting! Do you have any recommendations?

B：Absolutely! The almond croissant is my favorite. It's flaky and just the right amount of sweet. How about you, tried any favorites here?

A：这里的糕点看起来真诱人！你有什么推荐吗？

B：当然有！杏仁羊角面包是我的最爱。它既酥脆又甜得恰到好处。你呢，这里有没有特别喜欢的？

3.8.3 At a concert/event

(1) A：What a great turnout! Have you ever been here before?

B：No, this is actually my first time here. The atmosphere is amazing! How about you? Are you a regular?

A：人真多！你以前来过这里吗？

B：没有，这是我第一次来这里。气氛真棒！你呢？你常来吗？

（2）A：I'm really excited about the main act. Have you listened to their latest album?

B：Yes，it's been on repeat in my playlist！Especially the third track. Do you have a favorite song from them?

A：我对主要节目真的很期待。你听过他们的最新专辑吗？

B：是的，我一直在反复听！尤其是第三首歌。他们的歌曲中有没有你特别喜欢的吗？

3.8.4 At a playground

（1）A：My kids are sure full of energy today！

B：I can see that！It's great to see them having so much fun.

A：我的孩子们今天真是精力充沛！

B：看得出来！看到他们玩得这么开心真好。

（2）A：Swings seem to be a timeless favorite for children，don't they?

B：Absolutely！My child could spend hours on it. How old is your little one?

A：秋千似乎永远是孩子们的最爱，不是吗？

B：绝对是！我的孩子可以在上面玩几个小时。你的小家伙多大了？

Exercises

3-1 Write a brief paragraph discussing why the ability to start a conversation is crucial in a business setting.

3-2 Using the contexts provided，write a few lines to start a conversation.

（1）Starting a conversation with a friend you haven't seen in a long time.

（2）Starting a conversation with a colleague during lunch break.

（3）Starting a conversation with someone you were just introduced to at a conference.

（4）Starting a conversation with a stranger at a café.

3-3 Pair up with a classmate. One of you will choose a context from the list provided and initiate a conversation. The other person will respond. After a few lines of dialogue，switch roles.

Scenarios：

（1）Meeting an old friend at a wedding.

（2）Meeting a colleague at a work event.

（3）You're in a waiting room with a stranger.

（4）You bump into your boss at a coffee shop on the weekend.

（5）You've just been introduced to someone important in your industry.

（6）You're sharing an elevator ride with a colleague from another department.

3-4 Match the sentences in Column A with the appropriate situations in Column B related to starting a conversation.

Column A	Column B
（1）Long time no see！How have you been?	A. With someone you were just introduced to

(2) This is a great event, isn't it?	B. With someone you meet outside
(3) Hi, I believe we haven't met before. I'm Mike.	C. With a stranger at a café
(4) It's such a lovely day, isn't it?	D. At a conference/work event
(5) Excuse me, could I borrow the sugar?	E. With a friend you haven't seen in a long time

Unit 4 General communication

In daily life, effective communication is vital. This unit delves into common communication techniques and scenarios. We will learn how to offer suggestions and opinions, express preferences, discuss rules and regulations, and how to bid farewell appropriately. Additionally, we'll explore how to ask for help, decline others, apologize, and how to respond to both good and bad news. With these skills mastered, you'll be able to communicate with others comfortably in any situation.

日常生活中，有效沟通是至关重要的。本单元将深入探讨日常的交流技巧和场景。我们将学习如何提供建议和意见，表达喜好、讨论规章制度，以及如何恰当地告别。此外，本单元还将探讨如何请求帮助、拒绝他人、道歉，以及如何回应好消息或坏消息。掌握这些技巧后，无论在哪种情境下，你都能够自如地与他人交流。

4.1 Offering advice and suggestions

(1) I think **the weather is perfect for a picnic**.
我认为**这天气最适合野餐**。

(2) In my opinion, **reading is one of the best ways to expand one's horizons**.
在我看来，**阅读是拓宽视野的最好方法之一**。

(3) I'm (pretty) sure that **the movie starts at 8 pm**.
我（非常）确定**电影晚上 8 点开始**。

(4) As far as I'm concerned, **everyone should have the right to express their opinions freely**.
在我看来，**每个人都应该有自由表达意见的权利**。

(5) Why don't you **try a new hobby to keep yourself occupied**?
你为什么不**尝试一种新的爱好来让自己有事可做**呢？

(6) Have you thought about **joining a weekend workshop**?
你考虑过**参加周末工作坊**吗？

(7) Perhaps you/we should **reconsider our decision**.
也许你/我们应该**重新考虑我们的决定**。

(8) Why don't we **go to the new Italian restaurant downtown**?
我们为什么不**去市中心那家新开的意大利餐馆**呢？

(9) One idea/suggestion/alternative/option would be to **carpool to reduce our carbon emissions**.

一个想法/建议/替代方案/选择是**拼车以减少我们的碳排放**。

4.2 Likes/dislikes/preferences

(1) I love/like/really love/really like/quite like **chocolate**.
我爱/喜欢/真的爱/真的喜欢/非常喜欢**巧克力**。

(2) I don't mind **being vegetarian**.
我不介意**吃素**。

(3) I hate/loathe/can't stand/can't bear **getting up early**.
我讨厌/痛恨/受不了/不能忍受**早起**。

(4) I prefer **tea** to **coffee**.
与**咖啡**相比，我更喜欢**茶**。

(5) I'd prefer to **eat at home**.
我倾向于**在家里吃**。

(6) If I had the choice, I'd prefer/opt for/go for **a quiet beach vacation over a bustling city trip**.
如果我有选择，我倾向于/选择/去**安静的海滩度假，而不是繁华的城市旅行**。

(7) **Whether it's an apple or an orange**, it's all the same to me.
无论是苹果还是橘子，对我来说都一样。

(8) **Whether it's this restaurant or that one**, it's much the same to me.
无论是这家餐馆还是那家餐馆，对我来说都差不多。

(9) **Eating Chinese food or Western food**, I don't mind either way.
吃中餐还是西餐，我都不介意。

(10) **Chocolate flavor or vanilla**, either is fine by me.
巧克力味的或香草味的，我都可以。

4.3 Talking about rules and regulations

(1) I'm sorry, but for safety reasons, you're not allowed to **wear open-toed shoes in the laboratory**.
对不起，出于安全考虑，你在实验室内不允许**穿着露趾的鞋子**。

(2) I'm sorry, but you can't **smoke here**.
抱歉，你不能**在这里吸烟**。

(3) I'm sorry, but it's against office policy to **bring pets inside**.
抱歉，**把宠物带进来**违反办公室规定。

(4) I'm sorry, but as per building regulations, one can't **park vehicles in front of the emergency exit**.

抱歉，根据大楼规定，不可以在**紧急出口前停车**。

(5) I'm sorry, but the office rules are quite clear about this. Visitors can't **use mobile phones in the working area**.
抱歉，办公室对此有很明确的规定。访客不能**在工作区域使用手机**。

(6) I'm sorry, but due to health standards, we don't permit **outside food or drinks in the cafeteria**.
对不起，由于健康标准，食堂不允许带入**外部的食物或饮料**。

4.4 Saying goodbye

4.4.1 Complimenting

(1) You have a wonderful perspective, I've learned a lot from our discussions.
你的观点很好，从我们的讨论中我学到了很多。

(2) It is very nice to meet you.
很高兴见到你。

(3) I've really enjoyed our time together.
我真的很享受和你在一起的时光。

(4) Your insights and conversations have been truly enriching.
你的见解和谈话真的很有启发性。

4.4.2 Giving an excuse

(1) I wish I could stay, but I have to pick up my kids from school.
我希望我能留下，但我得去学校接我的孩子。

(2) Actually, I'd better be going since my train leaves in half an hour.
其实，我得走了，因为火车半小时后就要开了。

(3) I'd love to stay longer, but I have an early meeting tomorrow.
我很想多待一会，但我明天有一个早会。

(4) I need to leave now, I have another appointment in an hour.
对不起，我得走了，一小时后我还有个约会。

4.4.3 Making a promise

(1) I'll definitely attend your event next time; you have my word.
我下次一定会参加你的活动；我向你保证。

(2) So, I'll call you next time I'm in the area.
因此，下次我在这个地区的时候会给你打电话。

(3) I promise to return this book to you by the end of the week.
我保证在这周结束前把这本书还给你。

(4) I'll send you those details when I get back to the office.
我回到办公室后会把这些细节发给你。

4.4.4 Referring to a future meeting

(1) I'll send you an invitation to our annual event; hope to see you there.
我会给你发送我们年度活动的邀请；希望到时候能见到你。

(2) I look forward to seeing you at the next workshop.
我期待着在下次研讨会上见到你。

(3) Let's schedule a time to discuss this further next week.
我们约定下周找个时间进一步讨论这个问题。

(4) I would really like you to meet our managing director.
我真的希望你能见见我们的总经理。

4.4.5 Apologizing

(1) I sincerely apologize for the oversight; it won't happen again.
我真心为我的疏忽道歉；这种事不会再发生了。

(2) I'm sorry for cutting this short, I have another commitment I can't miss.
抱歉打断一下，我还有另一个不能错过的约会。

(3) I didn't mean to cause any inconvenience. Please accept my apology.
我不是故意造成不便的。请接受我的道歉。

(4) Please forgive me, I lost track of time and didn't mean to be late.
请原谅，我没注意时间，不是有意迟到的。

4.4.6 Thanking your host

(1) Your kindness and generosity have made my visit memorable. Thank you.
你的善意和慷慨使我难忘。谢谢你。

(2) Thank you for a lovely evening.
谢谢你给我一个美好的夜晚。

(3) I had a lovely time, thank you very much for your hospitality.
我过得很愉快，非常感谢你的款待。

(4) Thank you so much for the party, but I really have to be going now.
非常感谢你的派对，但我现在真的得走了。

4.5 Asking for help

(1) Could you help me?
你能帮我吗？

（2） Could you give me a hand with this?
你能帮我一下吗？
（3） Have you got a couple of minutes?
你有几分钟时间吗？
（4） Would you mind helping me with something?
你介意帮我个忙吗？

4.6 Saying no

4.6.1 Saying what you'd prefer

（1） A：Do you mind if I **smoke**? /Would you mind if I **opened the door**?
B：Actually，I'd rather you didn't. /Well，I'd prefer it if you didn't.
A：我**抽烟**你介意吗？/我**开门**你介意吗？
B：事实上，我宁愿你不要。/好吧，我希望你不要。
（2） A：Would it bother you if I **played music aloud**?
B：I'd appreciate it if you used headphones. /To be honest，I'd like it quiet right now.
A：如果我**大声播放音乐**会打扰你吗？
B：如果你用耳机，我会很感激的。/老实说，我想现在安静点。

4.6.2 Offering an alternative suggestion

（1） A：Can you work overtime this evening?
B：It's a bit difficult at such short notice，but I could work overtime tomorrow evening instead. Would that work for you? / That might be a bit difficult for me this evening，but I could do any other evening this week.
A：今晚你能加班吗？
B：临时接到通知有点困难，但我明天晚上可以加班。这样可以吗？/今晚对我来说可能有点困难，但这周其他任何一个晚上我都可以。
（2） A：Could you finish this task by the end of the day?
B：I have a tight schedule today，but I can prioritize it first thing tomorrow morning. Would that be alright?
A：你能在今天结束前完成这项任务吗？
B：我今天的日程很紧，但我可以明天早上先做它。这样可以吗？

4.6.3 Saying sorry

（1） A：Can you work late tonight?
B：I'm afraid I can't. /I'm really sorry，but I have something on tonight.
A：你今晚能加班吗？

B：恐怕不行。/很抱歉，我今晚另有安排。

（2） A：Would you be available for a meeting tomorrow morning?

B：I apologize，but I'm already committed to another appointment. /Sorry，I have a prior engagement at that time.

A：你明天早上有时间开会吗？

B：对不起，我已经有另一个会了。/抱歉，我那段时间已经约出去了。

4.6.4 Using alternative expressions

（1） A：Can I have a pay rise?

B：I'm not sure this will be possible this year. /I don't think we can offer you any more. /To be honest，that's going to be difficult. /Actually，no one is getting a pay raise this year.

A：我可以加薪吗？

B：我不确定今年是否有可能。/我想这方面目前没有上涨空间。/老实说，挺困难的。/事实上，今年没有人会加薪。

（2） A：Can I switch to a different department?

B：Given the team's current dynamics，I'm afraid it's not feasible at the moment.

A：我能换到别的部门吗？

B：考虑到团队目前的动态，恐怕现在不可行。

4.7 Apologizing

4.7.1 When you can't help someone

（1） A：Can I speak to Mike，please?

B：I'm sorry，he isn't in at the moment. /Hes out of the office today.

A：我可以和迈克讲话吗？

B：对不起，他现在不在。/他今天不在办公室。

（2） A：Can you assist with the server issue?

B：I'm sorry，that's outside my area of expertise. /Unfortunately，I'm not well-versed in that aspect.

A：你能帮忙解决服务器问题吗？

B：对不起，那不在我的专业范围内。/不巧，我不精通那方面。

4.7.2 When you want to disagree politely

（1） A：We should reorganize the sales department.

B：I'm sorry，but I disagree with you.

A：我们应该重组销售部门。

B：对不起，我不同意你的看法。

（2）A：The marketing strategy needs more offline campaigns.
B：I understand where you're coming from，but I respectfully disagree.
A：营销策略中需要更多的线下活动。
B：我理解你的考虑，但我不同意。

4.7.3 When you want to interrupt

（1）A：And so，to sum up，I think that we should，perhaps…
B：Sorry，can I say something here?
A：所以，总结一下，我认为我们应该，也许……
B：对不起，我能在这里说几句吗？
（2）A：As I was mentioning，the quarterly reports indicate that…
B：Excuse me，may I interject a point?
A：正如我刚才提到的，季度报告显示……
B：对不起，我可以插一句吗？

4.7.4 When you do something accidentally

（1）That was my mistake；I didn't intend for it to happen.
那是我的错；我不是有意为之。
（2）Oops，sorry.
哦，抱歉。
（3）My apologies，that was unintentional.
对不起，我不是故意的。
（4）Oh no，that wasn't on purpose. My apologies.
哦，不，我不是故意的。对不起。

4.7.5 When you don't understand

（1）I'm not quite sure what you mean. Can you clarify?
我不太确定你的意思。你能解释一下吗？
（2）Sorry，I don't follow you.
抱歉，我没听懂你的话。
（3）Can you explain that in simpler terms?
你可以用更简单的话解释一下吗？
（4）Sorry，can you repeat that，please?
抱歉，你能再说一遍吗？

4.7.6 When you keep someone waiting

（1）I didn't intend for this to take so long；thank you for your patience.
我没想到这事拖那么久；谢谢你的耐心。

(2) Sorry to keep you waiting.
抱歉，让你久等了。

(3) My apologies for the delay.
对不起耽误了你的时间。

(4) I appreciate your understanding, and I'm sorry for the wait.
感谢你的理解，抱歉让你久等了。

4.7.7 When you are in someone else's way

(1) Oh, sorry!
哦，对不起!

(2) My bad, I'll step aside.
我的错，我这就让开。

(3) Excuse me, my apologies for blocking your way.
对不起，很抱歉挡住了你的路。

(4) Pardon me, didn't realize I was in the way.
对不起，我没意识到挡住了你的路。

4.7.8 When you want to show sympathy

(1) I can't imagine how hard this must be for you; I'm here for you.
我无法想象这对你有多么困难；我会支持你的。

(2) I was really sorry to hear about your grandma's illness.
听说你奶奶病了，我真的很难过。

(3) My heart goes out to you during this difficult time regarding your grandma.
在你奶奶患病的困难时刻，我的心与你同在。

(4) Sending you my deepest condolences for your grandma's passing.
对你奶奶的逝世谨向你致以最深切的哀悼。

4.7.9 When you cause disruption or inconvenience to someone

(1) I apologize for the inconvenience, but we're currently undergoing maintenance.
抱歉给你带来不便，但我们目前正在进行维护。

(2) Sorry to be a nuisance, but the company's rules don't allow that.
抱歉打扰你，但公司的规定不允许这样做。

(3) My apologies for the noise; we're trying to fix the issue as soon as possible.
对于这噪声，我表示抱歉；我们正在尽快解决这个问题。

(4) I'm sorry, but you can't park here.
抱歉，你不能在这里停车。

4.8 Responding to good/bad news

4.8.1 Responding to good news

(1) Congratulations!
恭喜你!

(2) Good for you! You really deserve it!
为你感到高兴!你值得!

(3) That's excellent news!
真是个好消息!

(4) Fantastic!
太棒了!

(5) I'm really pleased for you.
我真为你高兴。

(6) That's wonderful news!
真是个好消息!

4.8.2 Responding to bad news

(1) Oh, I'm so sorry to hear that! /Oh, that's such a pity. /Oh, that's too bad.
哦,听到这个消息我很难过!/哦,那太遗憾了。/哦,那太糟糕了。

(2) That's heart-wrenching news. I'm here for support if you need any assistance during this time.
那是个令人心碎的消息。如果你在这段时间需要任何帮助,我都会支持你。

(3) I'm so sorry. Please let me know if there's anything I can do.
我很抱歉。如果有什么我能做的,请告诉我。

(4) Please accept my condolences.
请接受我的哀悼。

Exercises

4-1 Your friend is feeling stressed about an upcoming exam and isn't sure how to prepare. Write a short paragraph offering advice and suggestions on how they might best study and prepare.

4-2 Read the following situation: A colleague invites you to a party, but you can't attend because you accidentally double-booked with another event. Write a response to your colleague that includes:

(1) Politely declining the invitation (saying no);

(2) Apologizing for not being able to come;

(3) Responding positively to their news about a promotion they mention in their invitation.

4-3 Match the sentences in Column A with the appropriate situations in Column B related to the general communication.

Column A	Column B
(1) I've always had a fondness for early morning meetings.	A. Asking for help
(2) Before you leave, make sure to submit your reports as per department regulations.	B. Talking about rules and regulations
(3) It's hard to say farewell after all these years at the company.	C. Saying goodbye
(4) I'm not sure how to operate this new software. Can someone guide me?	D. Expressing a preference

4-4 Read the four choices marked A, B, C and D, and decide which is the best answer to each question.

(1) Jane told her boss that she prefers working from home on Fridays because ____.

A. she dislikes the office environment

B. there's a rule about it

C. it allows her to avoid rush hour traffic

D. she wants to say goodbye

(2) Why did the manager implement the new regulation on meeting etiquette? ____.

A. He wanted to say goodbye

B. He likes informal meetings

C. To ensure that meetings are more productive and streamlined

D. He needed to ask for help

(3) When leaving for her maternity leave, Sarah said to her team ____

A. "I dislike the office policy."

B. "Can someone assist me with these files?"

C. "I'll miss you all, take care!"

D. "The regulations are too strict."

(4) John is unsure about the procedure to request annual leave. He should ____.

A. say goodbye to his colleagues

B. discuss his preferences with his manager

C. ask HR or a colleague for assistance

D. dislike the rule

Unit 5 Job interviews

Job interviews are a pivotal moment in our professional journey. This unit aims to provide you with the skills and strategies to successfully navigate interviews. We will delve into common interview questions, clarify the dos and donts during interviews, assist you in making your answers more concise and compelling, guide you through the use of clear signposting language, and teach you how to effectively describe experiences using the STAR method. Furthermore, we'll instruct you on how to establish better communication and rapport with interviewers by mirroring key words. Mastering these techniques will enable you to approach interviews with greater confidence and significantly increase your chances of success.

求职面试是我们职业生涯中一个关键的环节。本单元旨在为你提供成功应对面试的技巧与策略。我们将深入探讨常见的面试问题，明确面试中的注意事项，使你的回答更加简洁有力，指导你使用清晰的路标词，引导你运用 STAR 法则有效地描述经验。此外，我们还将教授你如何通过镜像关键词与面试官建立更好的沟通与连接。掌握这些方法，将使你在面试中更加从容自信，大大增加成功的机会。

5.1 Common interview questions

(1) Tell me a little about yourself.
简要介绍下自己。

(2) What skills or experiences do you have that would make you successful in this role?
你有哪些技能或经验能让你在这个职位上取得成功?

(3) Where did you see yourself five years from now?
你觉得五年后的自己会是什么样子?

(4) What are your strengths/weaknesses?
你的优点/缺点是什么?

(5) What is your leadership style?
你的领导风格是怎样的?

(6) Can you tell me about a time when you demonstrated excellent customer services?
你能告诉我一个你为客户提供了优质服务的例子吗?

(7) Tell me about a time you dealt with a challenging situation at work.
请给出一个你在工作中应对挑战的例子。

(8) How do you think your values fit our company culture?
你认为你的价值观与我们公司文化的契合度如何?

(9) How do you handle stress and pressure at work?
你如何处理工作中的压力?

(10) How do you deal with feedback, both positive and negative?
你如何处理积极反馈和消极反馈?

(11) Why did you leave (or why are you leaving) your last job?
你为什么离开（或为什么计划离开）上一份工作?

(12) Why do you want this job?
你为什么想要这份工作?

(13) Why should we hire you?
我们为什么要雇佣你?

(14) What are you looking for in terms of salary?
你对薪水的要求是多少?

(15) Do you have any questions?
你有什么问题吗?

5.2 Interview do's and don'ts

5.2.1 Interview do's

(1) Research the company. Before your interview, ensure you are well-acquainted with the company's goals, history, culture, and the job role you are applying for. It shows you're serious and thoughtful.
研究公司。在面试前，确保你非常了解公司的目标、历史、文化及你申请的职位。这会显示出你是一个认真且深思熟虑的人。

(2) Prepare your responses. Think about questions you are likely to be asked and prepare thoughtful, concise answers. Use the STAR method (Situation, Task, Action, Result) for behavioral interview questions.
准备你的回答。想想你可能被问到的问题，准备周到、简洁的答案。对于行为面试的问题，使用 STAR 法则（情境，任务，行动，结果）。

(3) Arrive early. If the interview is in-person, plan to arrive about 10-15 minutes early. For online interviews, ensure your devices are working well in advance.
提前到达。如果是现场面试，计划提前 10~15 分钟到达。对于在线面试，提前确保你的设备运行良好。

(4) Dress appropriately. Always dress professionally and in accordance with the company's dress code. If in doubt, it's better to overdress than underdress.
穿着得体。始终要穿着专业，并符合公司的着装要求。如果拿不准的话，穿得太正式总比穿得太随便好。

(5) Bring necessary materials. Bring multiple copies of your resume, a list of references, and a notebook to jot down important details.

带上必要的材料。带上多份简历，一份推荐信，还有一个笔记本用来记下重要的细节。

(6) Show excitement and enthusiasm. Employers want to see that you're interested in the job and the company.

表现出兴奋和热情。雇主希望看到你对这份工作和公司感兴趣。

(7) Listen and respond accordingly. Too often the feedback from interviewer is that the candidate does not answer the question in a clear and direct manner. Don't run interviewers around the questions, listen and answer accordingly while using examples from your experience to back it up.

倾听并做出相应的回答。面试官的反馈往往是候选人没有以清晰直接的方式回答问题。不要在问题上绕圈子，倾听并做出相应的回答，同时用你经历过的案例来支持你的观点。

(8) Sell your strengths and expertise. Make sure that you communicate your strengths to the interviewer in a concise, factual and sincere manner.

展现你的优势和专长。确保你以一种简洁、真实和真诚的方式向面试官传达你的优势。

(9) Ask questions. Prepare insightful questions to ask at the end of the interview. This can demonstrate your interest in the role and help you decide if the job is a good fit for you.

提问。准备一些有见地的问题，在面试结束时提出。这可以表明你对这个职位的兴趣，并帮助你决定这份工作是否适合你。

(10) Send a follow-up thank you email. Send a thank you email to the interviewer expressing your appreciation for the opportunity. This can leave a positive, lasting impression.

发送后续感谢邮件。给面试官发一封感谢邮件，表达你对这次机会的感激。这能给对方留下积极、持久的印象。

5.2.2 Interview don'ts

(1) Don't show up late. Being late shows a lack of respect for the interviewer's time and may indicate potential time management issues.

不要迟到。迟到表明你不尊重面试官的时间，也可能表明你有潜在的时间管理问题。

(2) Don't mispronounce the names of those interviewing you. Double check the pronunciation of names with the receptionist or hiring manager prior to your interview. Getting names correct is a simple matter of courtesy and respect.

不要把面试官的名字念错。面试前和接待人员或招聘经理核实面试官名字的发音。正确地说出名字是基本的礼貌和尊重。

(3) Don't speak negatively about present or previous employers. Keep the conversation positive. Speaking poorly about present or past employers can make you come across as unprofessional.

不要说现任或前任雇主的坏话。保持对话积极。说现任或前任雇主的坏话会显得你不专业。

(4) Don't interrupt the interviewer. Allow them to finish their thoughts and questions before you answer. Interrupting can come off as rude and impatient.
不要打断面试官。等他们说完他们的想法和问题再回答。打断别人会显得粗鲁和没耐心。

(5) Don't lie. Honesty is crucial in job interviews. Don't inflate your skills or qualifications; it's better to be upfront about what you don't know and emphasize your willingness to learn.
不要说谎。在求职面试中，诚实是至关重要的。不要夸大你的技能或资格；最好坦率承认自己不懂的东西，强调自己学习的意愿。

(6) Don't forget body language. Don't slouch, cross your arms, or avoid eye contact. These non-verbal cues can make you appear uninterested or unfriendly.
不要忘记肢体语言。不要驼背、交叉双臂，或避免眼神接触。这些非语言暗示会让你显得不感兴趣或不友好。

(7) Don't be too casual. Maintain a professional tone throughout the interview. Avoid using slang or overly familiar language.
不要太随意。在整个面试过程中保持专业的语气。避免使用俚语或过于亲近的语言。

(8) Don't let any past rejections infringe on future ones. Finding a new job can be taxing, make sure you approach every interview as a new opportunity and learn from past interview mistakes. If you have several interviews lined up, try to leave some space between them to ensure you are at your best.
不要让过去的失利影响到未来。找一份新工作可能会很费力，确保你把每次面试都当作一个新的机会，并从过去的面试失误中吸取教训。如果你有几个面试排在一起，试着在它们之间留出一些时间，以确保你处于最佳状态。

(9) Don't discuss salary or benefits too early. If the interviewer brings it up, then it's fine to discuss. But asking too early can give the impression that you're only interested in the compensation, not the job itself.
不要过早讨论薪水或福利。如果面试官提出，那就可以讨论。但是问得太早会给面试官留下这样的印象：你只对薪酬感兴趣，而不是工作本身。

(10) Don't leave without asking questions. Failing to ask questions may indicate a lack of preparation or interest in the role.
不要不问问题就离开。不问问题可能表示你对这个职位缺乏准备或兴趣。

Remember, every interview is a learning experience. Even if you don't get the job, you can learn from the experience and improve for future interviews.
记住，每一次面试都是一次学习的经历。即使你没有得到这份工作，你也可以从这次经历中学习，并为以后的面试作准备。

5.3　Making your answers more concise

5.3.1　Question: Tell me a little about yourself

Sample answer (Rambling)

Well, I was born in a small town in northern Italy, where I also went to school. I studied engineering at university and then… So, after I graduated… I mean, I did a masters degree first, but then I worked for a small firm in my hometown for a few years, which was great fun. After that…

⟶ *includes unnecessary details*
包含不必要的细节

⟶ *doesn't speak in full sentences*
没讲完整的句子

⟶ *doesn't have any clear direction*
没有明确的方向

Sample answer (Concise)

I've always loved designing and building things, so I suppose it's natural that I became an engineer. I've worked in a variety of roles and companies, which I've learned a lot from, but now I'm ready for a new challenge.

5.3.2　Question: Where did you see yourself five years from now?

Sample answer (Rambling)

There are many things I could be doing. I'd like to have, you know, some sort of progress… What I mean is that I don't just want to be doing the same things I'm doing now. I like to be moving forward in my career, for example … Err… I definitely see myself in a better position than I am now.

Sample answer (Concise)

I don't know exactly, but the most important thing is that I continue to learn and grow in my career. I'm the kind of person who needs new challenges to stay focused. I might even start my own business, because that's something I've always wanted to do at some point in my life.

5.4　Using signposting language

Signposting language means words and phrases which show your listener where you're going, and will make your answers clearer and more structured. For example, the phrase "for example" is

signposting language. When one says "for example", you know he/she is about to give you an example. Without signposting language, longer answers can lose focus and be hard to follow.
路标词是指向听众展示你思路的词汇和短语。它们会让你的回答更清晰、更有条理。例如，"例如" 就是路标词。当一个人说 "例如" 时，你知道他/她要给你举个例子。没有路标词，较长的回答可能会失去焦点，难以理解。

5.4.1 Question: What are your strengths/weaknesses?

Sample answer (No signposting language) 示例答案（无路标词）	Sample answer (Signposting language) 示例答案（有路标词）
I'm very good at working with other people. In my last job, I always tried to encourage my colleagues and create a good atmosphere. I suppose I can be a little bit careless sometimes. I'm not the kind of person who focuses on details. I'm very calm, and I can keep a cool head in very stressful situations.	**Firstly**, I'm very good at working with other people. **For example**, in my last job, I always tried to encourage my colleagues and create a good atmosphere. **On the other hand**, I suppose I can be a little bit careless sometimes, **because** I'm not the kind of person who focuses on details. **Coming back to strengths**, I'm very calm, and I can keep a cool head in very stressful situations. Signposting language: **Firstly**, **For example**, **On the other hand**, **because**, **Coming back to strengths**

5.4.2 Question: What is your leadership style?

Sample answer (No signposting language) 示例答案（无路标词）	Sample answer (Signposting language) 示例答案（有路标词）
I'm quite a hands-off manager. If one of my team has a project, I'll keep an eye on things, but I don't need to be involved in every detail. I'm very approachable. I make sure my team know they can come to me with problems or questions at any time. I like to lead from the front. If everyone's working late to meet a deadline, I make sure I'm there with them.	**First of all**, I'm quite a hands-off manager. **For instance**, if one of my team has a project, I'll keep an eye on things, but I don't need to be involved in every detail. I'm **also** very approachable, **in that** I make sure my team know they can come to me with problems or questions at any time. **Finally**, I like to lead from the front. **That means that** if everyone's working late to meet a deadline, I make sure I'm there with them. Signposting language: **First of all**, **For instance**, **also**, **in that**, **Finally**, **That means that**

5.5 STAR method

STAR means Situation, Task, Action and Result. So, you start your answer by giving the context: what was the situation, and what did you have to do? Then, you talk about what you actually did, and what the end result was.

STAR 是情境、任务、行动和结果的缩写。所以，你开始回答时先描述背景：是什么情境，你需要做什么？然后，谈论你实际做了什么，以及最终的结果是什么。

5.5.1 Question: Can you tell me about a time when you demonstrated excellent customer service?

Sample answer using STAR method 运用 STAR 法则的示例答案	Analysis of STAR method in sample answer 示例答案的 STAR 法则分析
There was one time when a customer's order hadn't arrived, and we didn't know what had happened to it. The customer was very unhappy, and I had to try to solve the problem for him. I arranged for a replacement to be sent, thinking we could find out what happened to the previous order later. In the end, the customer was happy that I could solve his problem quickly and simply.	**S**: There was one time when a customer's order hadn't arrived, and we didn't know what had happened to it. **T**: The customer was very unhappy, and I had to try to solve the problem for him. **A**: I arranged for a replacement to be sent, thinking we could find out what happened to the previous order later. **R**: In the end, the customer was happy that I could solve his problem quickly and simply.

5.5.2 Question: Tell me about a time you dealt with a challenging situation at work

Sample answer using STAR method 运用 STAR 法则的示例答案	Analysis of STAR method in sample answer 示例答案的 STAR 法则分析
Once, we realized three days before a project deadline that two of our teams were using incompatible software tools. As the project manager, I had to find a way to deal with this without causing any delays. I talked to both team leaders and we made a plan for one team to convert their work into a different format, with help from some staff from other departments.	**S**: Once, we realized three days before a project deadline that two of our teams were using incompatible software tools. **T**: As the project manager, I had to find a way to deal with this without causing any delays. **A**: I talked to both team leaders and we made a plan for one team to convert their work into

It was very close but we managed to get everything done on time.

a different format, with help from some staff from other departments.

R: It was very close but we managed to get everything done on time.

5. 6 Mirroring key words

5. 6. 1 Mirroring meaning

Mirroring means using some of the same or similar words and expressions as the person you're talking with
镜像是指和与你对话的人使用一些相同或相似的单词和表达。
For example:
Question: How do you think your **values fit** with our **company culture**?
Answer: I think my **values** are a good **fit** for your **company culture** for two reasons. One…
问：你认为你的价值观与我们公司文化的契合度如何？
答：我认为我的价值观很适合贵公司的文化，原因有二。首先……

5. 6. 2 Benefits of mirroring

(1) It keeps your answers focused. By using the same words and phrases, your answer will be relevant.
让你的回答有重点。通过使用相同的词汇和短语，使答案与问题相关。
(2) It shows the interviewer that you're listening and that you care about the questions and the company.
向面试官表明你在倾听，并且关心面试官提出的问题和公司情况。
(3) You unconsciously mirror people when you like or respect them. Using mirroring consciously will help you to make a better impression.
当你喜欢或尊重别人时，你会无意识地模仿他们。有意识地使用镜像词会帮助你留下更好的印象。

5. 6. 3 Considerations when applying for a company position

(1) Read the job advertisement carefully.
仔细阅读招聘广告。
(2) Find out how they describe themselves and what adjectives they use on their website or in their advertising.
了解公司如何描述自己，以及他们在网站或广告中使用了哪些形容词。
(3) Pay attention to the words they use to describe the candidate they're looking for.

注意公司用来描述理想候选人的词汇。

(4) Use these words in your answers.

在你的回答中使用这些词汇。

5.6.4 Using mirroring

Example 1. You're applying to a company which describes itself as innovative and forward-looking. In the job advertisement, they say they want someone who is creative and flexible.

例 1. 你正在申请一家自称具有创新和富有前瞻性的公司。招聘广告中说他们需要候选者有创意且灵活。

Question: Why do you want this job?

Sample answer: Creativity is very important to me, and I've always wanted to work in an environment where I can innovate and find my own solutions to challenges. I also feel that your company will continue to evolve in the future, and I like the idea of contributing to that development.

Note: The candidate doesn't use all four words, but she does reference all four ideas. For example, instead of forward-looking, she talks about the company evolving in the future. In this way, she shows that she's in tune with the company's values.

注意：候选人没有使用全部的四个词，但她确实提及了这四个要点。例如，她没有说前瞻性，而是谈到了公司未来的发展。通过这种方式，表明了她与公司的价值观是一致的。

Example 2. You're applying to a company which describes itself as "commanding respect" and which talks with pride about its long history. In the job advertisement, they say they want someone who has great communication skills and passion for helping others.

例 2. 你正在申请一家令人肃然起敬，历史悠久的公司。招聘广告中说他们需要候选者具有良好的沟通能力，且乐于助人。

Question: Why should we hire you?

Sample answer: I believe that great customer service starts with good communication, which is a strength of mine. I also think that in customer service, you need to care about what you're doing. I care about helping others and as such I believe you would find me to be a respectful and effective team member who can fit with the established traditions of your company.

Note: Again, the candidate doesn't necessarily use the words directly, but he does reference all four of the ideas. If you use mirroring method, don't sound like a robot. This is why you sometimes need to change words and phrases slightly, instead of repeating them again and again.

注意：同样，候选人没有直接引用这些词，但提到了全部的四个要点。如果你使用镜像方法，不要听起来像个机器人。这就是为什么你有时需要稍微改变词汇和短语，而不是一遍又一遍地重复它们。

Exercises

5-1 List five common job interview questions that employers often ask, and provide a brief, concise answer to each.

5-2 Use signposting language to answer the following interview question: Tell me about your previous experience and why you're interested in this role.

5-3 Use the STAR method to answer the following interview question: Can you describe a time when you solved a challenging problem at work?

5-4 Read the following job description and write down five key words or phrases that you could mirror in a job interview.

The ideal candidate is a team player, adaptable, and has a strong background in project management. Excellent communication skills and a problem-solving attitude are essential.

5-5 Pair up with another student. One person will act as the interviewer and the other as the candidate. The interviewer should ask questions based on the key words identified in Exercise 5 and the candidate should respond using the techniques learned in this unit.

5-6 Read the four choices marked A, B, C and D, and decide which is the best answer to each question.

(1) In a job interview, why is it important to make your answers concise? ____.

A. To display superior language skills

B. To ensure clarity and efficiency of communication

C. To minimize the interview duration

D. To avoid answering certain questions

(2) How might you demonstrate the ability to be concise in your answers during a job interview? ____.

A. By using complicated vocabulary and industry jargon

B. By repeating your points for emphasis

C. By delivering focused responses that directly address the questions

D. By diverting the topic away from the question

(3) Which of the following behaviors is NOT a method for keeping your answers concise during a job interview? ____.

A. Speaking quickly to fit in more information

B. Eliminating unnecessary details or tangents

C. Focusing on the main points related to the question

D. Using specific examples to illustrate points

(4) When preparing for an interview, what might be a strategy for ensuring your answers are concise? ____.

A. Rehearse possible questions and your answers

B. Plan to elaborate on every point you make

C. Aim to take up as much time as possible with each answer

D. Avoid using any examples or stories

(5) What's a potential drawback of providing answers that are too verbose during a job interview? ____.

A. The interview may lose focus on key points

B. The interviewer will be impressed by the amount of information

C. The interviewer will have more details to assess the candidate

D. The interview will last longer, indicating interest from the employer

Unit 6 Presentations

In this unit, we will delve into presentation skills. Meanwhile, you will learn how to properly introduce yourself and your topic, ensuring that your introduction captures the attention of your audience. Furthermore, we will introduce the use of signposting language to help you organize and present your content more effectively. Lastly, addressing common problems during the presentation will also be a focal point of this unit. Through this unit, you will be able to deliver business presentations with greater confidence.
在本单元中，我们将深入探讨演讲技巧。同时，你会学习如何恰当地介绍自己及你的演讲主题，确保你的开场白引人入胜，从而吸引听众的注意。此外，我们还会介绍路标词的使用，帮助你更有效地组织和呈现你的内容。最后，如何应对演讲中的常见问题也是该单元的重点内容。通过这个单元，你将能够更自信地进行商务场合的演讲。

6.1 Presentation tips

6.1.1 Choosing a topic that ignites your passion

If you can choose the topic, make sure it's one you're interested in and can be passionate about. Your passion will have a positive effect on your audience, will help them to focus and will make you more confident and relaxed. However, if you can't choose the topic, try to make it your own. Is there anything about it you can relate to, can you turn it into a story that you are excited to tell?
如果你可以选择演讲主题，请确保它是你感兴趣的主题并充满激情的。你的激情会对你的听众产生积极的影响，帮助他们集中注意力，也会让你更加自信和放松。如果不能选择主题，那么你可以试着找到一个独特的角度、观点或方法来处理，使其更贴近你的兴趣、经验或风格。有没有什么东西能让你产生共鸣，你能将它变成一个你乐于讲述的故事？

6.1.2 Writing your ideas down first

Before even considering slides, ensure you have all your ideas documented. Once they're on paper, organize them coherently. Spend time refining and drafting your content until it feels just right. Seek feedback from friends, family, or colleagues to further polish your script.
在考虑使用幻灯片之前，确保已将所有想法记录在案。一旦写在纸上，就要条理清晰。花时间完善和起草你的内容，直到感觉恰到好处。也可以向朋友、家人或同事寻求反馈，进一步完善你的讲稿。

6.1.3 Using structure to build on ideas

A disorganized presentation with scattered points can confuse your audience, making it memorable for the wrong reasons. Conversely, structuring your presentation so that each section logically builds upon the previous one aids your audience in grasping the content. Establishing these coherent connections between concepts simplifies intricate ideas, facilitating better understanding and retention for your listeners.

如果演讲内容杂乱无章，观点分散，就会让听众感到困惑，对其中的错误印象深刻。相反，利用结构框架来建立想法，使之环环相扣，逻辑严密，则有助于听众理解内容。在概念之间建立这些连贯的联系，可以简化复杂的观点，便于听众更好地理解和记忆。

6.1.4 Using visuals

Using visuals such as charts, graphs, and infographics in your presentation can effectively solidify concepts for your audience. Given that about 65% of individuals are visual learners, neglecting this method might mean overlooking a significant portion of your audience. Images, be they photos, graphs, or charts, can often communicate information more powerfully than words alone. As the adage goes, "a picture is worth a thousand words." Thus, minimize excessive text on your slides. Ensure readable font sizes and proofread for spelling, grammar, and punctuation errors.

在演讲中使用图表、图形和信息图表等视觉资料可以有效地为听众巩固概念。鉴于约65%的人是视觉学习者，忽视视觉资料可能意味着忽视了很大一部分听众。图像，无论是照片、图形还是图表，往往比文字更能有效地传达信息。俗话说："一图胜千言。"因此，尽量删减幻灯片上过多的文字。确保字体大小清晰可读，并校对拼写、语法和标点错误。

6.1.5 Knowing your audience and anticipating questions

Research your audience to customize your presentation to their needs. Understand their background and anticipate potential questions they might pose. Tailor your content to resonate with them.

研究你的听众，以便根据他们的需求定制你的演讲。了解他们的背景，预测他们可能会提出的问题。调整你的内容，与他们产生共鸣。

6.1.6 Taking a self-recording

Record yourself delivering the presentation using a video camera or smartphone. Review the footage to assess your body language and vocal quality. Are you excessively moving? Fidgeting with your hands? Does your voice lack variation? Pay attention to your intonation, does your voice fluctuate appropriately? Are you pausing as intended?

用摄像机或智能手机录下自己的演讲。查看录像，评估自己的肢体语言和声音质量。是否存在动作过多？手忙脚乱？声音是否单调？注意语调，声音是否适当地起伏？是否按计划停顿？

6.1.7 Arriving early and checking equipment

Allocate ample time to reach the venue, familiarize yourself with the room, and understand its layout. Determine your standing position. Ensure that all the technical equipment is functioning properly. Check if assistance is available for setup if required.
安排充足的时间到达会场，熟悉会场，了解其布局。确定你的站立位置。确保所有技术设备正常工作。检查是否有必要的协助人员。

6.1.8 Having a clear beginning, middle and end

Begin by outlining your topic and explaining its significance to your audience. Delve deeper into your main points in the middle section. As you conclude, recap what you've discussed, reiterate its relevance, and leave a lasting impression. Conclude by expressing gratitude to your audience and welcoming any questions.
首先概述你的主题，并向听众解释它的重要性。在中间部分深入探讨你的主要观点。在结尾时，回顾一下你所讨论的内容，重申其相关性，加深听众对内容的印象。最后，向听众表示感谢，欢迎他们提出任何问题。

6.1.9 Using pauses

Pauses enable your audience to absorb your message and maintain focus on your presentation. Taking a 1-2 second break indicates you're transitioning from one topic to the next. After posing a rhetorical question or sharing a startling fact, allow for a brief 1-2 second pause. To ensure you incorporate them at the right moments, consider noting down these pauses in your script or notes.
停顿可以让听众吸收信息，保持对演讲的关注。1~2 秒的停顿表示你正在从一个话题过渡到下一个话题。在提出一个反问或分享一个令人震惊的事实后，可以有 1~2 秒的短暂停顿。为了确保你在适当的时机加入这些停顿，可以考虑在讲稿或笔记中标记出这些停顿。

6.2 How to introduce yourself and your topic

Imagine you're standing in front of your colleagues. You need to introduce yourself and what your presentation is about. What are some words and phrases you could use?
想象一下，你正站在同事面前。你需要介绍自己及演讲内容。你可以使用哪些单词和短语？

6.2.1 Introducing yourself

6.2.1.1 Formal

(1) Good morning everyone. For those who don't know me, my name's Mike, and I work in the marketing department.

大家早上好。先向初次见面的同事介绍下我自己，我叫迈克，在市场部工作。

(2) Hello everybody. Before we begin, let me introduce myself briefly: I'm Julia and I'm the head of HR.
大家好。在我们开始之前，让我简单介绍一下我自己：我是茱莉亚，人力资源部的主管。

6.2.1.2 Informal

(1) Hi guys; if you don't know me, I'm Mike and I work in digital marketing.
大家好；如果你们不认识我，我是迈克，从事数字营销工作。

(2) Hello! I see some new faces, so I'll introduce myself first: I'm Julia and I'm one of our customer service team.
大家好！我看到了一些新面孔，所以我先自我介绍一下：我是茱莉亚，是我们客户服务团队的一员。

6.2.2 Introducing your topic

6.2.2.1 Simple topic

(1) Today, I'm going to be talking about our new HR policies and how they affect you.
今天，我要讲的是我们新的人力资源政策及它们对你的影响。

(2) I'd like to talk to you today about quality control and why we're all responsible for quality control, whichever department you work in.
今天我想和大家谈谈质量控制，以及为什么无论你在哪个部门工作，都要对质量控制负责。

6.2.2.2 Complex topic

(1) I'll begin by outlining the policies, and then I'll go on to highlight what they mean for you and your working habits. Finally, I'll briefly discuss why we feel these new policies are necessary and beneficial for us all.
我先概述一下这些政策，然后再强调它们对你和你工作习惯的意义。最后，简要讨论为什么我们认为这些新政策对我们所有人都是必要且有益的。

(2) First of all, I'll explain why quality control has a broader meaning than you might expect. I'll continue by giving examples of real quality control, and why this matters for all of us. To finish, I'll be asking you to think of ways you can incorporate quality control into your working habits.
首先，我将解释为什么质量控制的含义比你想象得要广泛。我将继续给出真实的质量控制的例子，并解释为什么这对我们所有人都很重要。最后，我会请你们思考如何将质量控制融入你们的工作习惯。

6.3 How to make a strong start

In your life, you might have heard good speakers and bad speakers.
在你的生活中，你可能见过好的演讲者和糟糕的演讲者。

6.3.1 Differences between good speakers and bad speakers

6.3.1.1 Good speakers

(1) Good speakers understand that no one has to listen to them, so they work hard to make you want to pay attention.
好的演讲者明白没有人必须听他们的演讲，所以他们会努力赢得听众的关注。

(2) Good speakers grab your attention and don't let go. You want to hear what they say. You feel interested and energized by listening to them.
好的演讲者会抓住你的注意力，不会让你分心。你想听他们说些什么。听了他们的演讲，你会感到兴趣盎然、精神振奋。

6.3.1.2 Bad speakers

(1) Bad speakers are the opposite, and they don't think they have to earn your attention.
糟糕的演讲者恰恰相反，他们不认为自己需要赢得你的注意。

(2) Even if you try to make yourself listen, you find that your attention drifts away. Your eyelids feel heavy, and you have to struggle to stay awake.
即使你努力让自己倾听，你也会发现自己的注意力不集中。你会感到眼皮沉重，不得不努力保持清醒。

(3) What does this mean for you, and your presentation? You need to make it clear what people should expect from your presentation, and why they should care about what you have to say. Sounds like a nice idea, but how do you do this?
这对你和你的演讲意味着什么？你需要弄清楚人们应该从你的演讲中期待什么，以及为什么他们应该关心你要说的内容。弄清楚这些会帮助你成为好的演讲者，但是要怎么做呢？

6.3.2 Three techniques

6.3.2.1 Problem →solution

Establish a problem which many people in your audience have. Then, establish that you have a solution to their problem.
确定一个许多观众都想解决的问题。然后，向他们展示你有解决这个问题的办法。

For example

(1) Have you ever felt unfairly treated at work, or felt that the work you do isn't appreciated? We've been working to design new HR policies that will make sure all staff get fair recognition for their contribution to the company.
你是否曾经在工作中感到被不公平对待，或者你的工作没有得到赏识？我们一直在努力设计新的人力资源政策，以确保所有员工对公司的贡献得到公平的认可。

(2) In this way, you take a boring-sounding topic like HR policies, but you make it more relevant to your audience. How? By connecting it with their experiences and feelings.
通过这种方式，你可以把一个听起来很无聊的话题，比如人力资源政策，变得与听众更加相关。怎么做呢？可以通过将其与他们的经历和感受联系起来。

6.3.2.2 Interesting facts or statistics

Mention an interesting fact, or a surprising statistic to get people's attention.
提及一个有趣的事实或令人惊讶的统计数据来引起人们的注意。

For example

Did you know that the average office worker spends eight hours a day at work, but only does four hours of productive, useful work? I'm here to tell you about "quality control", and how you can use this idea to make better use of your time.
你知道上班族平均每天工作 8 小时，但只有 4 小时是高效、有用的工作吗？我来和你们讲讲"质量控制"，以及如何利用这个理念更好地利用时间。

6.3.2.3 Short stories

Finally, you can engage people by telling a short story and connecting it to your topic. Stories are powerful, and they can add an emotional dimension to your topic if you do it well.
最后，你可以讲一个与你的主题相关联的小故事来吸引人们。故事有强大的感染力，如果讲得好，还能为你的主题增添情感色彩。

For example

(1) I once met a young salesman, I won't mention his name. He spent several weeks building a relationship with a potential client. He worked overtime, and he was working so hard that he was under severe stress, which started to affect his personal life. In the end, he didn't close the deal-the clients signed with another firm. Today, I'm going to talk about confidence as a sales tool, and how you can avoid the traps that this young man fell into.
我曾经遇到一个年轻的推销员，我就不提他的名字了。他花了几个星期的时间与一位潜在客户建立关系。他加班加点，工作非常努力，压力很大，这开始影响到他的个人生活。最后，他没有做成这笔生意，客户和另一家公司签约了。今天，我要谈谈如何将自信作为一种销售工具，以及如何避免这个年轻人掉进陷阱。

(2) Use one of these three techniques in your introduction to connect with your audience and show them why they should be interested in what you have to say.
在介绍中使用这三种技巧中的一种来与你的听众建立联系，并向他们展示为什么他们应该对你要说的话感兴趣。

6.4 Using signposting language

Having interesting or relevant information is not enough. How you structure and organize your information is equally important. If you don't structure your presentation clearly, people won't pay attention. So, how can you do this? You use signposting language. This means using words and phrases to show the audience where your points begin and end, to show what's coming next, and to remind them about things you talked about before.
拥有有趣或相关的信息还不够。如何架构和组织信息也同样重要。如果你的陈述结构不清晰，人们就不会注意。那么，怎么做呢？使用路标词。即使用单词和短语来向听众说明你的观点从哪里开始，在哪里结束，说明接下来要讲什么，并提醒听众你之前讲过的内容。

(1) Okay, that covers the new policies. **Next**, I'd like to move on and discuss what these policies mean for you.
好的，新政策就讲到这里了。**接下来**，我想继续并讨论一下这些政策对你们意味着什么。

(2) **Now that** you've heard a bit about what not to do, **let's focus on** positive advice to help you be more effective salespeople and close more of your leads.
既然你们已经了解了不应该做的事情，**让我们把重点放在**积极的建议上，来帮助你们成为更有效的销售人员，并获取更多的潜在客户。

(3) **Next**, I'd like to talk about…
下面，我想谈谈……

(4) **Let's move on** and discuss…
让我们继续讨论……

(5) At this point, I'd like to **turn to**…
在这一点上，我想**转到**……

(6) Let me go into some **more details** about…
让我**详细**谈一谈……

(7) Let's examine… **in more depth**.
让我们**更深入地**研究……

(8) I'd like to **elaborate on**…
我想**详细说明**……

(9) **To wrap up**, let's remind ourselves of why this should matter to everyone here.
最后，让我们提醒自己为什么这对在座的每个人都很重要。

(10) **Let's review** the key points from this session.
让我们回顾一下这次会议的要点。

(11) So, you've heard what I said. **What conclusions** can you take away from this?
好了，你们已经听完了我说的内容。从中你们能得出**什么结论**呢？

6.5 Dealing with problems

6.5.1 Common problems

(1) Forget where you were.
忘记你说到哪里了。

(2) Forget an important word.
忘记一个重要的词。

(3) Realize that you said something wrong.
意识到自己说错了。

(4) Didn't explain something clearly.
没有解释清楚。

(5) Forget to mention something important.
忘记提及重要的事情。

(6) Someone might ask you an awkward question, which you have no idea how to answer.
有人可能会问你一个尴尬的问题，你不知道如何回答。

(7) Other possibilities.
其他可能性。

6.5.2 Advice and language for dealing with problems

(1) If you lose your place, and can't remember what to say next, you can use a filler phrase.
如果你失去了思路，不记得下一步该说什么，你可以使用填充短语。
Where was I?
我说到哪儿了？
So, what was I saying?
我刚才说什么来着？
What's the word in English again?
那个词用英语怎么说来着？

(2) It's a good idea to make a cue card with key points, as well as any important vocabulary you need. If you lose your place, or you forget a word, it could help.
最好制作一张提示卡，写上要点和所需的重要词汇。如果你失去了思路，或者忘词了，它可以帮到你。

(3) If you forget something, it's better to keep talking, rather than just standing there in silence.
如果你忘记了什么，最好继续说下去，而不要只是沉默地站在那里。

(4) What if you make a mistake, or you realize that you didn't explain something well? You could say:
如果你犯了一个错误，或者意识到你没有很好的解释好某件事情怎么办？你可以说：
Let me rephrase that.
让我换个说法。
Actually, what I meant to say is...
其实，我的意思是……
To clarify, I wanted to say that...
澄清一下，我想说的是……

6.5.3 Coping methods when you realize that you forgot to mention something important

(1) Let me just add one more thing: ...

让我再补充一点：……

（2）I'd like to add something to a point we discussed earlier.
我想对我们之前讨论过的一个问题做一些补充。

（3）Let me return to an earlier point briefly.
让我简单地回顾一下前面的问题。

6.5.4 The 3Ds options for handling difficult question：delay，deflect，dismiss

6.5.4.1 Delay giving an answer

（1）I've allocated time for questions at the end of this session，so we'll address your idea later.
我在本场会议的最后预留了提问时间，我们稍后再讨论你的想法。

（2）I'm not in a position to answer that right now，but I'll get back to you later this week.
我现在不能回答这个问题，但我会在本周晚些时候回复你。

6.5.4.2 Deflect the question

（1）That's an interesting question. Before I answer，I'd like to know：what's your take on this?
这是个有趣的问题。在我回答之前，我想知道：你对此有何看法？

（2）You've raised an important point there. What does everyone else think about this?
你提出了一个很重要的观点。其他人对此有什么看法？

6.5.4.3 Dismiss the question

（1）Thanks for your input，but I don't see how that's connected to what I'm saying.
谢谢你的意见，但我不认为这与我所说的有什么联系。

（2）I don't mean to be blunt，but I don't think that's relevant to today's discussion.
我不想失礼，但我认为这与今天的讨论无关。

Exercises

6-1 Introduce yourself informally，and explain your topic in a simple way，with one sentence when making a presentation. Then，introduce yourself formally，and explain your topic in a more detailed way.

6-2 Which technique would you prefer to use，and why，to introduce your topic and get people's attention from the beginning of your presentation?

6-3 Do you have any advice for giving good presentations，in English or any language?

Unit 7　Chairing a meeting

Chairing a meeting is a crucial aspect of business communication. This unit will guide you in efficiently presiding over meetings. Firstly, we will introduce some words and phrases pertinent to meetings. Following that, you'll learn how to start a meeting, clarify its objectives, advance the agenda effectively, invite participants to join the discussion, offer opinions, and handle distractions to ensure the discussion remains on-topic. Lastly, we will teach you how to summarize the meeting's content and conclude it appropriately. With these skills mastered, you'll be able to lead any meeting smoothly and methodically, ensuring its objectives are achieved.

主持会议是商务沟通中的重要环节。本单元将指导你高效主持会议。首先，我们会介绍一些与会议相关的词汇和短语。之后，你将学习如何开始会议，明确会议目的，高效推进议程，邀请与会者参与讨论，提供意见，以及如何应对会议中的干扰并确保讨论始终与主题相关。最后，我们会教你如何总结会议内容并妥善结束会议。掌握这些技能后，你将能够有条不紊地主持任何会议，确保达到会议目标。

7.1　A few words and phrases

(1) **Have**: We're going to **have** another department meeting on Friday.
星期五我们还要**开**一个部门会议。

(2) **Hold**: Let's **hold** a meeting to discuss the policy changes.
我们**开**会讨论一下政策的变化吧。

(3) **Schedule**: Please **schedule** a meeting with the project team to discuss the progress of the work.
请**安排**一次与项目组的会议，以讨论工作的进展情况。

(4) **Arrange**: Can you **arrange** a meeting with our new clients to discuss the details of the upcoming project?
你能**安排**与我们的新客户会面，讨论一下即将进行的项目细节吗?

(5) **Organize**: It's your responsibility to **organize** the weekly team meeting and ensure all pertinent members are invited.
你有责任**组织**每周的团队会议，并确保所有相关成员都被邀请。

(6) **Go to**: Did you **go to** the project team meeting?
你去**参加**项目组会议了吗?

(7) **Attend**: Several people did not **attend** the development meeting.
有几个人没有**参加**开发会议。

(8) **Agenda**：A well-organized meeting will have an **agenda**，that's a list of topics that will be discussed in some meetings.
一个组织良好的会议会有一个**议程**，也就是会议将要讨论的主题清单。

(9) **Meeting minutes**：One person keeps notes that will be the official record of the meeting-these are called the **meeting minutes**.
由一个人做笔记记录会议内容，这份材料被称为**会议纪要**。

(10) **Brainstorm**：One reason to hold a meeting is to **brainstorm**. Brainstorming is creating a lot of different ideas，so that they can later be analyzed，evaluated，and the best ones can be selected.
开会的一个原因是**头脑风暴**。头脑风暴指创造许多不同的想法，以便稍后对它们进行分析、评估，并选择最好的想法。

(11) **Strategy/allocate tasks**：Another reason to hold a meeting is to develop a **strategy** and **allocate tasks**. A **strategy** is a plan for completing a project，and to **allocate tasks** means to assign specific items of work to specific people.
召开会议的另一个原因是制定**策略**和**分配任务**。**策略**是完成一个项目的计划，而**分配任务**意味着将特定的工作项目分配给特定的人。

(12) **Collaborate/updates**：Meetings are also held to **collaborate**（work together）on projects and give **updates**，reports of progress and current status.
召开会议也是为了在项目上**合作**（一起工作），并为进度和当前状态提供**更新**报告。

(13) **Make decisions**：Finally meetings are held to **make decisions**.
最后召开会议来**作决策**。

(14) **Voting**：Some meetings use a formal system of **voting** in which a decision is made if it receives the majority（more than 50%）of the votes.
有些会议采用正式的**投票**制度，如果获得多数（超过 50%）的投票，则决策通过。

(15) **Consensus**：Other meetings use a less formal system of decision-making aiming for the group to come to a **consensus** that means a general agreement.
有些会议采用的决策体系正式程度较低，目的是让参会者达成**共识**。

7.2 Starting a meeting

7.2.1 Getting people's attention

(1) If I could have your attention，please.
请大家注意听我说。

(2) Could/May I have your attention，please?
请大家注意一下，好吗？

(3) Good afternoon，everyone.
大家下午好。

(4) Good morning everyone. Could I have your attention please? (combination of two phrases)
大家早上好。请大家注意一下好吗?(两个短语的组合)

(5) Let's all settle down and focus.
让我们都安静下来,集中注意力。

(6) Can I get your eyes and ears for a second?
你能看着我并听我说一会儿吗?

(7) If you could give me your full attention.
如果你能全神贯注地听我说话。

7.2.2 Welcoming attendees

(1) I'd like to welcome you all here today. Now let's get down to business.
欢迎各位今天来到这里。现在我们开始谈正事吧。

(2) Thank you all for coming. Perhaps we can make a start.
谢谢大家的光临。也许我们可以开始了。

(3) Thanks everyone and welcome to today's meeting. Let's begin.
谢谢大家,欢迎参加今天的会议。让我们开始吧。

(4) Hello, everyone. Thank you for coming today.
大家好。感谢大家今天的到来。

(5) Since everyone is here, let's get started.
既然大家都到了,我们开始吧。

(6) First I would like to welcome you all.
首先,我想欢迎大家。

7.2.3 Introducing new people

(1) Let me bring to your attention our newest member of the team, Julia Jones, who will be heading our Marketing department.
请允许我为大家介绍我们团队的最新成员茱莉亚·琼斯,她将领导我们的市场部。

(2) I'd like to take a moment to introduce Mike Turner, our new director of operations.
我想花一点时间来介绍我们的新任运营总监迈克·特纳。

(3) Please join me in welcoming Dr. Mike turner. Dr. Mike turner is a highly respected neuroscientist.
请和我一起欢迎迈克·特纳博士。迈克·特纳博士是一位备受尊敬的神经科学家。

(4) Julia, would you like to introduce yourself?
茱丽亚,你想介绍下自己吗?

7.3 Stating the objective

(1) As you can see from the agenda, we'll be talking about the upcoming product launch strategies in the meeting.

正如你从议程中看到的，我们将会讨论即将推出的产品的发布策略。

(2) I've called this meeting in order to discuss and finalize the quarterly budget allocations.
我召集这次会议是为了讨论并确定季度预算分配。

(3) Our main goal today is to identify the challenges and solutions for improving our customer satisfaction ratings.
我们今天的主要目标是确定挑战和解决方案，以提高我们的客户满意度评级。

(4) The aim of this meeting is to evaluate the progress of our ongoing projects and determine the next steps for each team.
这次会议的目的是评估我们正在进行的项目的进展，并确定每个团队的下一步工作。

(5) In today's meeting, we'll go over the feedback received from our latest marketing campaign and discuss potential improvements.
在今天的会议中，我们将会讨论从我们最近的营销活动中收到的反馈，并讨论潜在的增长。

7.4 Getting through the agenda

7.4.1 Introducing the first agenda item

(1) First up, we need to discuss our upcoming product launch.
首先，我们需要讨论我们即将推出的产品。

(2) So, let's start with some new business: marketing strategies.
那么，让我们从一些新的业务：营销策略开始。

(3) Let's kick things off by addressing the feedback from last month's client survey.
让我们首先处理上个月客户调查的反馈。

(4) The first item on the agenda is how we can make our online advertising more effective.
议程上的第一项是如何使我们的在线广告更有效。

7.4.2 Moving between agenda items

(1) I think that covers the first/second/third item.
我想这涵盖了第一项/第二项/第三项。

(2) If nobody has anything else to add, we can continue on to the next item.
如果没有其他要补充的，我们可以继续下一项。

(3) Let's move on to the next item: the marketing budget for these new strategies.
让我们继续下一项：这些新策略的营销预算。

(4) Now we come to the main challenge: how to get 100,000 new contacts in the next few months.
现在我们来讨论主要的挑战：如何在接下来的几个月里获得10万个新联系方式。

(5) The final item on the agenda is to welcome our new hires: Mike in Finance and Julia in HR.
议程上的最后一项是欢迎我们的新员工：财务部的迈克和人力资源部的茱莉亚。

7.5 Inviting attendees to participat

7.5.1 Asking for opinions

(1) Julia, what's your opinion on this?
茱莉亚，你对此有什么看法?

(2) Would you like to share your thoughts on this question?
你能分享你对这个问题的想法吗?

(3) Could you add anything to our ideas here?
你能补充一下我们的想法吗?

(4) What are your thoughts/views about this scheme?
你对这个方案有什么想法/看法?

(5) I'd like to get your feedback on the new marketing strategies we've implemented over the past quarter.
我想听听你对我们上个季度实施的新营销策略的意见。

(6) What does everyone think about the proposed changes to our project management approach?
大家对我们项目管理方法的拟议变更有什么看法?

7.5.2 Handing over to another attendee

(1) Mike, would you like to introduce this item?
迈克，你能介绍一下这个项目吗?

(2) I'd like to hand it over to Julia who is going to lead in the next point.
我想把它交给茱莉亚，她将主讲下一部分。

(3) Alright, now Mike will have the floor.
好了，现在由迈克发言。

(4) Julia, given your involvement in this project, it would be great if you could introduce this topic.
茱莉亚，鉴于你参与了这个项目，如果你能介绍一下这个话题就太好了。

(5) Julia, you've had hands-on experience with this issue. Can you shed some light on it for us?
茱莉亚，你对这个问题有过亲身体会。你能为我们解释一下吗?

(6) Julia, can you provide an overview of the next agenda item for everyone?
茱莉亚，你能为大家概述下一个议程项目吗?

(7) Next, Mike is going to tell us about the latest updates on the project and the milestones we've achieved so far.
接下来，迈克将为我们带来项目的最新进展和迄今为止我们的里程碑式成就。

7.6 Giving opinions

7.6.1 Giving your opinions

Strong

(1) I strongly believe that...
我坚信……

(2) I'm positive that...
我肯定……

(3) I'm convinced that...
我确信……

(4) I have no doubt whatsoever that...
毫无疑问……

(5) There's no question that... (strongest)
毫无疑问…… (最强)

Normal

(1) I think/believe/feel that...
我认为/相信/感觉……

(2) From my point of view...
从我的角度看……

(3) In my experience.../I find that...
根据我的经验……/我发现……

(4) I'd say that...
我要说……

(5) If you want my honest opinion, I think that.../To be honest...
如果你想听我说实话，我认为……/说实话……

Weak

(1) It seems to me that...
对我来说似乎……

(2) It's possible that...
有可能……

(3) I tend to think that...
我倾向于认为……

(4) My initial reaction is...
我的初步反应是……

7.6.2 Agreeing

Strong

(1) I completely agree.
我完全同意。

(2) I couldn't agree more.
我非常同意。

(3) You're absolutely right.
你绝对是对的。

Normal

(1) Exactly!
完全正确！

(2) That's just how I see it.
这正是我的看法。

(3) I'm with Mike on this.
在这点上，我同意迈克。

Partial

(1) Well, it depends.
嗯，这得看情况。

(2) I agree with you up to a point, but...
我在某种程度上同意你，但是……

(3) I agree with you in principle, but...
我原则上同意你，但是……

7.6.3 Disagreeing

Strong

(1) I'm sorry, but I completely disagree.
对不起，我完全不同意。

(2) I'm sorry, but I don't agree with that at all.
对不起，我一点都不同意那样。

Normal

(1) I'm afraid I disagree.
恐怕我不同意。

(2) I'm not so sure about that.
对此我不太确定。

(3) I see it differently.
我的看法不同。

(4) Yes, but...
是的，但是……

(5) Not necessarily.
不一定。

7.6.4 Settling a disagreement

(1) Can we look at the issue from a different angle or perspective?
我们能从另一个角度或观点看待这个问题吗？

(2) We don't seem to be getting anywhere with this, so maybe we could discuss it further at another time.
我们似乎在这件事上没有任何进展，因此我们也许可以下次再进一步讨论。

(3) Let's both take a step back and see if there's another solution we haven't considered.
我们都退后一步，看看是否有其他尚未考虑的解决方案。

(4) Let's move on. I think we're going to have to agree to disagree.
我们继续吧。我想我们得求同存异。

7.6.5 Suggestions

Strong

(1) I suggest...
我建议……

(2) I recommend...
我推荐……

(3) We should...
我们应该……

(4) Let's...
让我们……

Weak

(1) We could...
我们可以……

(2) Why don't you/we...?
你/我们为什么不……？

(3) How about...?
对于……怎么样？

(4) What about...?
对于……怎么样？

Note：

（1） We could/Why don't we/We should/Let's + base form：
我们可以/我们为什么不/我们应该/让我们 + 动词原形：
We could **invest** in new technology.
我们可以投资新技术。

（2） How about / What about/I suggest/I recommend + ing：
怎么样/对于……怎么样/我建议/我推荐 + 动名词：
How about **investing** in new technology?
投资新技术怎么样？

7.6.6 Interrupting

（1） May I have a word?
我能说句话吗？

（2） Could I just say one thing?
我能说一件事吗？

（3） Excuse me，sorry for interrupting，I believe we need to prioritize discussing the upcoming product launch in today's meeting.
对不起，打扰一下，我认为我们今天的会议需要优先讨论即将推出的产品。

（4） Before you continue，can I make a quick point?
在你继续之前，我能简单说一点吗？

7.7 Dealing with distractions and staying on topic

7.7.1 Interrupting politely

（1） Let's not get too far off-topic here.
我们不要跑题太远。

（2） We can discuss that at the end if you feel it's important.
如果你觉得这很重要，我们可以在最后再讨论。

（3） I don't think that's relevant to today's discussion.
我认为那与今天的讨论无关。

（4） I think we've spent enough time on this topic. Moving on，let's address the budget concerns for the next quarter.
我想我们在这个话题上花的时间已经够多了。接下来，让我们讨论下一季度的预算问题。

（5） If nobody has anything else to add，let's move on to the next item.
如果没有什么要补充的，那我们就继续下一项。

(6) We're running short on time, so let's move on.
我们时间不多了，所以让我们继续吧。

(7) I'd like to skip item two and go directly to item three.
我想跳过第二项，直接看第三项。

(8) I'm afraid that's outside the scope of this meeting.
恐怕那不在这次会议的讨论范围之内。

(9) I think we're getting a bit off topic.
我想我们有点跑题了。

(10) Let's get back on track, OK?
让我们回到正题，好吗?

(11) Getting back to our discussion on the "Integration of Digital Marketing Strategies to Enhance Customer Engagement in the Third Quarter".
回到我们关于"第三季度整合数字营销策略以增强客户参与度"的讨论上来。

7.7.2 Moving a topic to another day

(1) Due to time constraints, let's revisit this topic in our next session.
因为时间限制，我们下次会议再回顾这个话题。

(2) I think we should shelve that until next time.
我想我们应该把这个问题放到下次讨论。

(3) Good point, but let's table it until the next meeting.
说得好，不过我们还是把它搁置到下次会议吧。

(4) We'd better save that for another meeting.
我们还是下次会议再讨论吧。

7.8 Summarizing and closing the meeting

7.8.1 Summarizing

(1) Before we close, let me just summarize the main points.
在我们结束之前，让我简要总结一下主要内容。

(2) To sum up...
总之……

(3) In brief...
简而言之……

(4) Shall I go over the main points?
我需要复述一下要点吗?

(5) Use verbs like discussed, went over and talked about.
使用动词如：讨论了、仔细讨论了、谈论了。

For example:

To sum up, we **discussed** using the new internet marketing strategies and cutting the budget by $1,000 next month. We also **talked about** our new sales goals and increasing our traffic. Finally, we welcomed Mike and Julia to the company.

7.8.2 Closing

(1) It looks like we've covered the main items for the meeting today.
看起来我们今天的会议已经涵盖了主要议题。

(2) Right, that's all for today's meeting.
好的，今天的会议到此结束。

(3) Is there any other business?
还有其他事项要讨论吗?

(4) Are there any questions before we finish?
在我们结束之前有任何问题吗?

(5) If no one has anything else to add, then I think we'll wrap this up.
如果没有其他人要补充，那我认为我们可以结束了。

(6) I'll let you know the date of our next meeting.
我会告诉你们下次会议的日期。

(7) Our next meeting will be/Let's get together...
我们的下次会议将在……/让我们……再讨论

For example:

Right, that's all for today's meeting. Are there any questions before we finish? No? Great, I'd like to thank Mike, our CEO, for coming here all the way from Beijing. Thank you all for attending. That's all for today.

Exercises

7-1 Imagine you're chairing a meeting at your company.

(1) Write down three agenda items.

(2) Practice using different English phrases to introduce each item.

7-2 How would you handle distractions during a meeting to ensure the discussion remains on topic? Provide an example scenario and your approach to dealing with it.

7-3 Match the phrases in Column A with the appropriate concepts in Column B related to chairing a meeting.

Column A	Column B
(1) On today's agenda we have...	A. Why important
(2) The main purpose of this meeting is...	B. Starting a part of the meeting
(3) Let's stay focused on the topic at hand.	C. Ending a meeting

(4) In conclusion, we have decided...
(5) I value your insights; can you share your thoughts?
(6) It's vital we address this issue today.
(7) I believe that...
(8) Thank you all for your contributions.
(9) We'll kick off with the first item.

D. Stating the objective
E. Getting through the agenda
F. Inviting attendees to participate
G. Giving opinions
H. Dealing with distractions and staying on topic
I. Summarizing and closing the meeting

7-4 Read the four choices marked A, B, C and D, and decide which is the best answer to each question.

(1) Why is it crucial for the chairperson to start a meeting effectively and state its objective? ____

A. To ensure everyone gets a chance to speak.

B. To make the meeting longer.

C. To set a clear direction and purpose for the discussion.

D. To show authority and power.

(2) Which phrase is best suited for a chairperson to use when they want to transition to the next item on the agenda? ____

A. I think we're getting off track.

B. Moving on to the next point...

C. In my personal opinion...

D. Mike, could you say something about this topic?

(3) When inviting attendees to share their views during a meeting, which phrase would be most appropriate? ____

A. I disagree with that perspective.

B. Let's skip this part.

C. I'd like to hear from [Name + Department].

D. This isn't relevant to our discussion.

(4) How should a chairperson handle distractions during a meeting? ____

A. By ignoring them and hoping they go away.

B. By addressing them briefly and redirecting the discussion back to the topic.

C. By ending the meeting immediately.

D. By asking the attendees for their opinions on every distraction.

(5) What phrase could a chairperson use to bring a conversation that has gone off-topic back on track? ____

A. This is not interesting, let's move on.

B. We seem to have strayed from the main point. Let's refocus on our agenda.

C. Can we discuss this later?

D. I don't see the relevance of this discussion.

(6) When summarizing the meeting's key points, the chairperson should ____

A. offer their personal opinion on each topic discussed.

B. briefly restate the main decisions made and tasks assigned.

C. speak only about the topics they found most interesting.

D. let attendees volunteer to summarize instead.

(7) Which phrase is most appropriate for a chairperson to use when they want to encourage a quieter member

to share their opinion? ____

A. Why haven't you spoken yet?

B. Julia, we'd love to hear your thoughts on this.

C. Please contribute, or we'll move on.

D. If you have nothing to add, just let us know.

(8) Dealing with distractions during a meeting is important because ____

A. it allows for more breaks during the meeting.

B. it ensures the meeting concludes on time with its objectives met.

C. it provides entertainment for the attendees.

D. it gives the chairperson a chance to showcase their leadership skills.

(9) In a situation where two attendees are disagreeing and causing a disruption, the chairperson should ____

A. let them continue until they resolve their differences.

B. ask them to continue the discussion offline and refocus the meeting.

C. decide immediately in favor of one attendee.

D. ask other attendees to vote on who is right.

Unit 8 Negotiation

In the business context, effective negotiation is crucial. This unit will guide you on how to establish your position, set terms, and how to set boundaries when disagreements arise. We will also explore how to reach an agreement satisfactory to both parties, and how to summarize and restate key information. Mastering these points will help you handle business communications more adeptly and navigate various negotiation scenarios with ease.

在商务场合，有效的谈判是至关重要的。本单元将指导你如何确立自己的立场，设定条件，以及在出现分歧时如何设定界限。我们还将探讨如何达成令双方满意的协议，并总结及重述关键信息。掌握这些要点，将帮助你在商务交流中更加得心应手，轻松应对各种谈判场景。

Scenario: A will role-play as the manufacturer's representative, while B will role-play as a purchaser for a shoe wholesaler and will be negotiating a deal. All the dialogues in this unit are conducted in this context.

情境：A 将扮演制造商的代表，而 B 将扮演鞋类批发商的采购员，并进行交易谈判。本单元的所有对话都是在这个背景下进行的。

8.1 Establishing your position

At the beginning of a negotiation, both sides need to make their position clear.

在谈判开始时，双方都需要明确自己的立场。

8.1.1 Stating what you want directly

(1) I suggest starting small and scaling up later.
我建议先从小做起，然后逐步扩大规模。

(2) We're thinking of starting with around 600 units per SKU.
我们考虑从每个 SKU 大约 600 件开始。

(3) We'd prefer to keep things flexible to begin with.
我们希望事情一开始就保持灵活性。

(4) I suggest a seven-month contract to begin with.
我建议先签一个 7 个月的合同。

(5) We're thinking of opening new branches in 10 cities.
我们打算在 10 个城市开设新的分公司。

(6) We'd prefer to do the marketing work ourselves.
我们更倾向于自己做市场营销工作。

8.1.2 Asking the other side specific questions to find out what they need

(1) What kind of volumes/schedule are you looking at?
你的需求量/计划是什么?

(2) What's the situation regarding production and delivery/minimum order volume?
生产和交货/最小订购量方面的情况如何?

8.1.3 Using open-ended questions to check information

(1) What do you have in mind exactly?
你到底有什么想法?

(2) And that would be per-month, or...?
是按月计算，还是……?

In the following dialogue, you will see several ways to do these.
在下面的对话中，你将看到这几种方法。

A: I've read your proposals, and I understand you're looking for unbranded shoes in a variety of styles.
我已经阅读了你的提议，了解你在寻找各种款式的无品牌鞋。

B: That's right.
是的。

A: Meaning sneakers, loafers, boots, sandals, and high heels, right?
是指运动鞋、休闲鞋、靴子、凉鞋和高跟鞋，对吗?

B: Correct.
没错。

A: Alright. So, my first question is: what kind of volumes are you looking at?
好的。那么，我的第一个问题是：你考虑的数量是多少?

B: Well, we're a reseller, so we rebrand the shoes and sell them on to retailers. We can potentially move quite a lot of product, but I suggest starting small and scaling up later. We're thinking of starting with around 600 to 1800 units per SKU (stock keeping unit), with more in popular sizes and colors.
嗯，我们是一家转售商，所以我们给鞋子重新打上品牌，然后卖给零售商。我们可能卖出很多产品，我建议先从小做起，然后逐步扩大规模。我们考虑从每个 SKU (最小库存单位) 600 件到 1800 件开始，流行的尺码和颜色会更多。

A: And that would be per-month, or...?
是按月计算，还是……?

B: We'd prefer to keep things flexible to begin with.
我们希望事情一开始就保持灵活性。

A: What do you have in mind exactly? I'm not against flexibility, but logistics require a certain amount of forward planning.
你到底有什么想法？我不反对灵活性，但物流需要一定的前瞻性计划。

B: Of course! Let me ask you something: what's the situation regarding production and delivery? How long does it take you to process orders?
当然！我想问你一些事情：生产和交货方面的情况如何？你们处理订单需要多长时间？

A: It's not completely fixed, but around two weeks. Larger orders can take more time.
不是完全固定的，大约两周。大订单可能需要更长时间。

B: That's fine, so here's our situation: we don't have a lot of warehousing space. That means we can't commit to a fixed schedule for deliveries. Instead, we'll have to make orders once our stock level is low enough and we have the space.
好吧，我们的情况是这样的：我们没有太大的仓储空间。这意味着我们不能保证一个固定的交货时间表。相反，我们必须在库存水平足够低，且有仓储空间时才下订单。

A: Hmm... That's possible. One thing you should know: we won't be able to offer the lowest prices if we can't be sure of your delivery schedule in advance.
嗯，那是可能的。有一件事你应该知道：如果我们不能提前确定你方的交货时间表，我们就无法提供最低价格。

B: I understand.
我明白。

A: And for one product category, for example sneakers, how many variations of size and color do you need?
对于一个产品类别，比如运动鞋，你需要多少种尺码和颜色？

B: We need all the common sizes, from 6 to 11, each in 17 colors.
我们需要所有常见的尺码，从 6 号到 11 号，每个尺码 17 种颜色。

8.2 Setting conditions

Very often, negotiations depend on setting conditions. What "you" can offer depends on what the other side can do.
谈判往往取决于设定条件。"你"能提供什么取决于对方能做什么。

8.2.1 If conditional clauses

(1) **If** we're ordering around 80,000 units at one time, what kind of per-unit pricing can you offer?
如果我们一次订购大约 8 万件，你能报的单价是多少？

(2) **If** we need higher volumes, would you be able to go lower?
如果我们需要更大的数量，你能降价吗？

(3) **If** we commit to a minimum volume over a six-month period, but with a flexible delivery schedule, could you offer us the same price?

如果我们承诺 6 个月的最低订货量，但交货时间灵活，你能提供相同的价格吗？

8.2.2 If conditional clauses with modal verbs in the main clauses

(1) **If** we commit to a longer contract, can you offer us a better price?

如果我们承诺签订一份有效期更长的合同，你能给我们一个更好的价格吗？

(2) **If** we agree to pay the licensing costs, would that make the deal work for you?

如果我们同意支付许可费用，这笔交易对你们来说可行吗？

8.2.3 Other ways to talk about conditions

(1) **Assuming** that you need a flexible schedule, we could offer eight dollars per unit for sneakers and loafers…

假设你需要一个灵活的时间表，我们可以提供运动鞋和休闲鞋每双 8 美元的价格……

(2) **Supposing** you could commit to a minimum monthly volume, we could go down to six and fifteen dollars.

假如你能承诺每月最低订货量，我们可以将价格降到 6.15 美元。

(3) **As long as** there were some limitations on the delivery timing, I think that would be acceptable.

只要在交货时间上有一些限制，我认为是可以接受的。

Let's see how to apply the phrases during a negotiation.

让我们来看看如何在谈判中应用这些短语。

B: OK, so **if** we're ordering around 80,000 units at one time, what kind of per-unit pricing can you offer?

好吧，**如果**我们一次订购大约 8 万件，你们能报的单价是多少？

A: That depends **if** you can commit to a regular delivery schedule or not. **Assuming** that you need a flexible schedule, we could offer 8 dollars per unit for sneakers and loafers, and 16 for boots and sandals.

那取决于你**是否**能承诺一个固定的交货时间表。**假设**你需要一个灵活的时间表，我们可以提供运动鞋和休闲鞋每双 8 美元的价格，靴子和凉鞋每双 16 美元的价格。

B: **If** we need higher volumes, would you be able to go lower?

如果我们需要更多的数量，你能降价吗？

A: Possibly, but the schedule is more important to us. **Supposing** you could commit to a minimum monthly volume, we could go down to six and fifteen dollars.

可能，但对我们来说时间表更重要。**假如**你能承诺每月最低订货量，我们可以将价格降到 6.15 美元。

B: **If** we commit to a minimum volume over a six-month period, but with a flexible delivery schedule, could you offer us the same price?

如果我们承诺 6 个月的最低订货量，但交货时间灵活，你能提供相同的价格吗？

A：**As long as** there were some limitations on the delivery timing, I think that would be acceptable.

只要在交货时间上有一些限制，我认为是可以接受的。

8.3 Disagreements and setting boundaries

If the other side makes a proposal which you can't accept, you can tell them directly.

如果对方提出的建议你不能接受，你可以直接告诉他们。

(1) We won't be able to offer you the lower price.
我们不能给你更低的价格。

(2) We can't offer our best prices without a regular commitment on your part.
没有你方的定期承诺，我们无法提供最优惠的价格。

(3) We're not willing to absorb those costs.
我们不愿意承担这些费用。

(4) I'll come right out and say that's not going to work for us.
我会直截了当地说，那对我们来说不可行。

(5) There's no way around this.
这是没有办法的事。

(6) I'm sorry but I have to draw a line here.
抱歉，但我必须在这里划清界限。

Let's see how to apply the phrases during a negotiation.

让我们来看看如何在谈判中运用这些短语。

A：Let's work out the details about delivery and scheduling. For us to make this work at the lower price, we'd need to have monthly deliveries, but we could let you adjust the size of the order to some extent, so that you can manage your warehousing space.

我们来讨论一下交货和日程安排的细节问题吧。为了使价格更低，我们需要每月交货，但我们可以让你方在一定程度上调整订单的数量，这样就可以管理你方的仓储空间。

B：**I'll come right out and say that's not going to work for us.** Flexibility is essential for us; our whole model is based on just-in-time logistics, so **there's no way around this**.

我就直说了，那对我们来说不可行。灵活性对我们来说很重要；我们整个模式都基于即时物流，**这是没有办法的事**。

A：Well, in that case, **we won't be able to** offer you the lower price. I have no problem with flexible deliveries as such, but **we can't** offer our best prices without a regular commitment on your part.

好吧，那样的话，**我们就不能**给你更低的价格了。我对灵活交货没有问题，但没有你方的定期承诺，**我们无法**提供最优惠的价格。

B：I'm sorry to be blunt, but this seems a little short-sighted on your part. We're potentially

looking to order millions of units each year. Flexible delivery doesn't mean that we won't place orders regularly, it just means that we need to control the timing and quantities.
抱歉直言不讳，但你方这样做似乎有点目光短浅。我们希望每年能订购数百万件。灵活交货并不意味着我们不会定期下订单，只是意味着我们需要控制时间和数量。

A：I understand completely, but you need to realize that we have our own logistics issues to deal with. If we don't know exactly when and how big an order will be, that creates costs for us. **We're not willing to** absorb those costs; I feel that if you need this flexibility, then you should be willing to pay for it. **I'm sorry but I have to draw a line here**. It's simply too risky for us to give you what you're asking.
我完全理解，但是你方应该意识到我们有自己的物流问题要处理。如果我们不能确切地知道订单的时间和数量，那对我们来说就会产生成本。**我们不愿意**承担这些费用；我觉得如果你方需要这种灵活性，那么你方应该愿意为此支付。**抱歉，但我必须在这里划清界限**。对我们来说，满足你方的要求太冒险了。

B：It seems like we've reached a bit of an impasse. Shall we take a ten-minute break?
看来我们陷入了僵局。我们休息 10 分钟好吗？

A：Good idea.
好主意。

8.4 Reaching agreement

When you've reached an impasse, you need to make suggestions so that you can move forward.
当你陷入僵局时，你需要提出建议以便继续前进。

8.4.1 Introducing a new idea

(1) I have a proposal which I hope can make this work for everyone.
我有一个提议，希望大家都能接受。

(2) Here's my solution: …
我的解决方案是：……

(3) I'll make another offer…
我再开个价……

8.4.2 Asking for new ideas

(1) What's your idea?
你的想法是什么？

(2) What would you suggest?
你有什么建议吗？

8.4.3 Reacting to new ideas

(1) That's a good offer.
这个报价很好。

(2) I think this should be feasible.
我认为这应该是可行的。

Next, let's see how to resolve disagreements in a productive way through dialogue.
接下来，让我们看看如何通过对话以富有成效的方式解决分歧。

A: Right, I've spoken to a few people, and I have a proposal which I hope can make this work for everyone.
好的，我已经和几个人谈过了，我有一个提议，希望大家都能接受。

B: Sounds good! What's your idea?
听起来不错！你的想法是什么？

A: The problem for us is that if you don't maintain a certain monthly volume, we might lose money at the lower prices, which obviously we can't do.
我们面临的问题是：如果你方不能保持一定的月订货量，我们可能会因较低的价格而赔钱，这显然是我们不能做的。

B: Sure.
当然。

A: So, here's my solution: we have a 16-month contract with a flexible delivery schedule, but with a minimum volume per-quarter. At the end of the quarter, if you haven't met the volume requirements, you're liable for the difference in price between your orders and the minimum.
因此，我的解决方案是：我们签一个 16 个月的合同，交货时间灵活，但每季度有最低订货量。在季度末，如果你方没有达到数量要求，就有责任支付你方订单与最低订货量之间的差价。

B: I like the basic idea, but earlier I suggested a seven-month contract, and this sounds like a much worse deal for us.
我喜欢这个基本想法，但之前我建议签订一个 7 个月的合同，听起来这对我们来说是一个更糟糕的交易。

A: Well, I want to make this work, but the lower prices only work if we can guarantee orders over a full year. **I'll make another offer**: you pay six-seventy-five dollars for button-up shirts and polo shirts, and fifteen-fifty dollars for jackets and overcoats. Then, you can have a seven-month contract, with minimum volume per-quarter.
好吧，我想做成这件事，但最低价格只有在我们能保证一整年的订单情况下才实施。**我再开个价**：有纽扣的衬衫和 polo 衫每件 6.75 美元，夹克和大衣每件 15.50 美元。然后，你可以签订一个 7 个月的合同，每季度有最低订货量。

B: **That's a good offer**, but can we have the minimum over the whole period, just to have more flexibility?
这个报价很好，但我们能不能在整个周期内有最低订货量，以便获得更多的灵活性？

A: I can't make more concessions than I already have, I'm afraid. I think this is a good compromise which allows us to move forwards.
恐怕我不能再做更多的让步了。我认为这是一个很好的折中方案，可以使我们向前推进。

B: I'll need to call my team to confirm, but **I think this should be feasible**.
我需要打电话给我的团队来确认，但**我认为这应该是可行的**。

A: Great!
很好!

8.5 Summarizing and restating

Once you've managed to reach an agreement, you should summarize what you've agreed, and then outline the next steps what you both need to take. You might also mention points which need to be discussed later.
一旦你们达成了协议，你应该总结一下协议的内容，然后概述你们双方都需要采取的下一步行动。你也可以提到以后需要讨论的要点。

To summarize what you've agreed, you could say:
要总结一下协议的内容，你可以说:

(1) Let's go through the main points: …
让我们回顾一下要点:……

(2) Regarding delivery/the pricing/the timetable, …
关于交货/定价/时间表，……

(3) We still need to settle the exact details of…
我们还需要确定……的确切细节。

(4) We still need to settle the exact details of the training program.
我们还需要确定培训计划的确切细节。

(5) There's also the matter of integration with our existing software systems.
还有与我们现有软件系统集成的问题。

(6) We'll put this in writing.
我们会把这个写下来的。

(7) We'll send you a provisional agreement.
我们会寄给你一份临时协议。

(8) We can work on getting a contract drawn up.
我们可以着手起草一份合同。

Next, let's see how to summarize and restate at the end of a negotiation.
接下来，让我们看看如何在谈判结束时进行总结和重述。

A: Let's go through the main points: you'll order a minimum of 600,000 units in a seven-month period, at a price of six-seventy-five dollars for button-up shirts, polo shirts, and fifteen-fifty dollars for jackets and overcoats.

让我们回顾一下主要要点：你方在 7 个月内最少要订购 60 万件，有纽扣的衬衫和 polo 衫的价格是 6.75 美元，夹克和大衣的价格是 15.50 美元。

B：That's right.
没错。

A：Regarding delivery，orders are flexible. However，you must commit to giving us at least four weeks'notice for each order.
订单的交货时间是灵活的。但是，你方必须承诺每笔订单至少提前 4 周通知我们。

B：Yes. We still need to settle the exact details of sizes，colors，and so on.
是的。我们仍然需要确定尺寸、颜色等确切细节。

A：Of course，but from our point of view，that isn't an issue. Production costs are almost identical.
当然，但从我们的角度来看，这不是问题。生产成本几乎相同。

B：OK，so we can work that out later.
好的，我们以后再解决这个问题。

A：There's also the matter of penalties in case you don't meet your minimum volume over the course of the contract...
如果你方在合同期内没有达到最低订货量，还有处罚的问题……

B：I thought we agreed that we would simply pay the unit cost for the shortfall?
我们不是已经同意只支付不足件数的成本吗？

A：Yes，but which unit cost? We need to agree separate minimums for the button-up shirts and polo shirts，and for the heavier items.
是的，但是哪一种件数成本呢？我们需要为有纽扣的衬衫和 polo 衫，以及较重的物品达成单独的最低订单量。

B：True，but I don't see that being a problem.
没错，但我不认为这有什么问题。

A：No，me neither. So，we'll put this in writing and send you a provisional agreement within the next few days. If everything looks OK，we can work on getting a contract drawn up.
对，我也这么认为。那么，我们将把这份协议写成书面形式，并在几天内寄给你一份临时协议。如果一切看起来都没问题，我们可以着手起草一份合同。

B：Perfect!
完美!

Exercises

8-1 Scenario：Art gallery exhibition space negotiation

Background：EmergingArtist is an up-and-coming contemporary artist who has recently gained a lot of attention in the local art scene. CityGallery，a well-known gallery in the city，has shown interest in hosting a solo exhibition of EmergingArtist's work. The artist and the gallery director have scheduled a meeting to discuss and finalize the terms of the exhibition.

Issues at stake:

- Duration and dates of the exhibition.
- Financial terms (commission percentage, rental fees, etc.).
- Promotion and marketing responsibilities.
- Sale and display conditions (e. g., framing, insurance, and presentation).

Questions:

(1) Establishing your position: "Given my recent recognition and the uniqueness of my pieces, I believe a two-month exhibition during the peak art season would be most beneficial for both of us. What is CityGallery's perspective on this?"

(2) Setting conditions: "For this exhibition, I'm looking at a 30–70 commission split in my favor and would like CityGallery to handle the majority of the promotional efforts. Is this feasible for CityGallery?"

(3) Disagreements and setting boundaries: "I've heard that previously, some artworks at CityGallery were displayed without adequate lighting and protection. I'm quite particular about how my art is presented. How can we ensure that my pieces will be displayed under the conditions I specify?"

(4) Reaching agreement: "I'm glad we're aligning on most terms. If we can agree on having a dedicated marketing campaign with at least three promotional events during the exhibition, I believe we can finalize this. Does that work for CityGallery?"

(5) Summarizing and restating: "To summarize, we're looking at a two-month exhibition with a 30–70 commission split, primary promotional efforts by CityGallery, specific display conditions for my art, and a commitment to three promotional events. Have I captured our discussion accurately?"

8-2 Read the four choices marked A, B, C and D, and decide which is the best answer to each question.

(1) The two sides have not come to an agreement. They are still ____.

A. deadly B. successful C. deadlocked D. negotiating

(2) It is doubtful that the parties will come to an agreement. There is little hope of a ____.

A. changing B. breakthrough C. collaboration D. resolution

(3) A: So, neither party is willing to ____? B: No. Neither one will make concessions.

A. complement B. compromise C. retain D. relent

(4) There is ____ in our position, which means we have not changed our position.

A. no change B. not a change C. no changing D. no alteration

(5) Negotiations are at an ____, which means the parties are unable to come to an agreement.

A. impact B. impart C. impasse D. inclination

(6) When negotiations ____, it means that they are continuing, but in an uncertain/difficult manner.

A. progress B. advance C. proceed D. waver

(7) When will this agreement ____, i. e., start/become valid/begin to operate?

A. come into effect B. come to effect

C. have an effect D. null and void effect

(8) We hope to ____ an agreement by Friday.

A. come B. restore C. reach D. go

(9) The talks broke down. It means the talks ____.

A. fell B. collapsed C. fell down D. terminated

(10) Both sides are hoping for a successful ____.

A. outcome B. outburst C. change D. conclusion

Unit 9 Communicating with your manager

Effective communication with your superior manager is a pivotal aspect of professional development. This unit emphasizes the importance of building trust and respect, how to manage workload and deadlines, and ways to navigate sensitive situations. We'll also explore strategies for addressing when things go wrong, expanding your roles and responsibilities, and adeptly approaching topics of pay raises and promotions. Lastly, we'll delve into resigning and the situation of being laid off. Mastering the skills of this unit will help foster a more harmonious and efficient relationship with your superiors.
与上级经理有效沟通是职业发展中的关键环节。本单元着重建立信任和尊重的重要性，如何管理工作量和应对截止日期，以及如何处理敏感情境。我们还将探讨当事情出错时如何应对，如何扩大你的职责范围，以及如何妥善处理加薪和晋升的话题。最后，我们会讨论如何辞职及面对被解雇的情境。掌握本单元的技巧，将帮助你与上级建立更和谐、有效的关系。

9.1 Building trust and respect

9.1.1 Six communication strategies

(1) Make suggestions, rather than orders 提建议，而不是下命令

Would it be possible to reschedule our meeting for tomorrow? rather than I want our meeting moved to tomorrow.

是否可能将我们的会议改到明天？而不是我想把我们的会议改到明天。

Could we explore the idea of implementing a feedback system? rather than We need to change and have a feedback system.

我们可以探讨一下建立反馈系统的想法吗？而不是我们需要做出改变并建立一个反馈系统。

May I suggest using a different material for better durability? rather than I think you should change the material.

我可以建议使用另一种更耐用的材料吗？而不是我认为您应该更换材料。

(2) Use hypotheses to make a business case 利用假设提出商业案例

If we do this, we might cut our overheads/reduce customer waiting times.

如果我们这样做，可能会削减我们的管理费用/减少客户的等待时间。

Handling our public relations could cut costs/enhance profit margin.
处理好我们的公共关系可以降低成本/提高利润率。

We might be able to reduce our expenditure/expand our customer base if we outsourced sales/attended exhibitions.
如果我们外包销售/参加展览，也许可以减少开支/扩大客户群。

(3) Use polite modal forms 使用礼貌的情态动词

Could I schedule a time for a meeting?
我可以安排一个会议的时间吗？

Is it alright if I begin work slightly late tomorrow?
我明天稍微晚一点开始工作可以吗？

May I leave earlier today?
今天我可以早点走吗？

(4) Use past tenses for significant requests 为重要的请求使用过去式

I was wondering if we could discuss a pay raise/if I could get some training.
我想知道我们是否可以讨论一下加薪/我是否可以得到一些培训。

I was hoping to apply for a promotion.
我想申请升职。

I was thinking of presenting the project in a different way, but would appreciate your opinion.
我想用另一种方式来展示这个项目，但希望您能提出意见。

(5) Be honest 坦诚

I don't have that information currently, but I'll retrieve it and update you soon.
我目前没有这些信息，但我会检索并很快向您提供最新信息。

I'll need to verify that and return to you.
我需要核实一下，然后回复您。

Actually, I don't have the costings/the sales figures yet, but I can get them next Monday.
事实上，我还没有成本/销售数据，但下周一我可以拿到。

(6) Being open 开放的态度

Would you mind taking me through your thinking here?
你介意跟我说说你的想法吗？

Could you elaborate on why you think this approach is the best option for our team?
你能详细说明为什么你认为这种方法是我们团队的最佳选择吗？

Why are you concerned about the sales figures/the stock levels rather than long-term industry trends/the shareholder's meeting?
为什么你关心的是销售数字/库存水平，而不是长期的行业趋势/股东大会？

9.1.2 Finding out about your manager's communication/management style

(1) How would you like me to update you on my work? Do you like regular meetings, or are daily or weekly emails more suitable?

您希望我如何向您汇报我的工作？您喜欢定期开会，还是每天或每周发邮件更合适？

(2) What items would you like me to send to you for review and approval?
您希望我将哪些项目发送给您审核和批准？

(3) How do you prefer I check in or report my progress to you?
您希望我如何向您汇报或报告我的进展？

(4) If I encounter challenges, would you like me to approach you directly, or is there another person I should consult?
如果我遇到挑战，您是希望我直接找您，还是有其他我应该咨询的人？

(5) How often do you like to give feedback?
您愿意多久给一次反馈？

(6) Could you share your primary expectations for me in this position?
您能分享您对我在这个职位上的主要期望吗？

(7) What objectives would you like me to achieve in this role?
您希望我在这个职位上达到什么目标？

9.1.3 Seeking feedback

(1) Would you spare a moment to talk about my work so far?
您能抽时间谈谈我目前的工作吗？

(2) Would it be possible to get your insights on my performance in this role?
能不能请您谈谈我在这个职位上的表现？

(3) I'd really appreciate your opinion on how I'm doing in the role.
我很想听听您对我的工作表现的看法。

(4) Do you have any particular concerns about how I'm doing?
您对我的表现有什么特别担忧的吗？

(5) Are there any improvements you'd like me to make?
您希望我做哪些改进？

(6) Are you satisfied with my work, or are there specific areas you'd like me to concentrate on?
您对我的工作满意吗？还是有什么特定的领域需要我专注？

9.1.4 Responding to feedback

(1) Thank you for telling me this. It's valuable guidance for my improvement.
谢谢您告诉我这件事。这对我的进步是宝贵的指导。

(2) That's obviously something that I need to change. Thank you for letting me know.
这显然是我需要改变的地方。谢谢您告诉我。

(3) Thank you for your input. My recent method didn't yield the desired results, so I'll work on a new strategy.
谢谢您的建议。我最近的方法没有达到预期的效果，所以我将制定一个新策略。

(4) I understand your point of view. How can I go about changing it?
我理解您的观点。我该如何去改变它呢？

(5) I understand. But could you give me some advice for doing it better/changing my approach?
我明白。但是您能给我一些建议让我做得更好/改变我的方法吗?

(6) Thank you for pointing that out. How should I handle this situation in the future?
谢谢您指出这一点。今后我应该如何处理这种情况?

9.2 Managing workload and deadlines

9.2.1 If your manager gives you too much work

(1) While I recognize the significance of all these tasks, it's becoming challenging to manage them simultaneously. Which should be my top priority?
虽然我认识到所有这些任务的重要性,但同时管理它们变得越来越具有挑战性。哪一项应该是我的首要任务?

(2) Currently, my primary focus is on acquiring new sales leads.
目前,我首要的关注点是获得新的销售线索。

(3) Would it be possible to get some help from Julia at the Marketing Department?
我可以从市场部的茱莉亚那里得到一些帮助吗?

(4) I've been deeply involved in marketing recently, but it seems to divert me from my core duties.
最近我全身心地投入市场营销工作中,但它似乎使我偏离了我的核心职责。

(5) Would it be possible for me to concentrate 100% on marketing/drop market research?
我可以100%专注于市场营销/放弃市场研究吗?

(6) I've got my hands full with multiple projects.
我手头有好几个项目要做。

9.2.2 When your manager gives you impossible deadlines

(1) I expect to complete this work by next week. However, the site redesign might require additional time.
我预计下星期能完成这项工作。不过,重新设计网站可能需要额外的时间。

(2) We typically finalize the year-end accounts within three to four days. However, considering the changes you're asking for, it might extend by a week or two.
我们通常在三到四天内完成年终决算。不过,考虑到您要求的更改,可能会延长一两个星期。

(3) If we stick to this tight deadline, we'll have to compromise on the product launch. Is that still OK with you?
如果我们坚持这个紧迫的截止日期,我们将不得不在产品发布上做出让步。您同意吗?

(4) That could be difficult unless I stop work on the lead generation.
这可能很困难，除非我停止开发新一代产品。

9.2.3 When your manager asks you to work overtime and you can't

(1) My contract is for 40 hours per week, and I'm unable to extend my availability beyond that.
我的合同规定每周工作 40 小时，我无法在那之外延长工作时间。

(2) I'm committed to the hours we initially agreed upon, and I won't be available for extra work currently.
我遵守我们最初商定的工作时间，目前我不能提供额外的工作。

(3) I'm afraid I can't work any extra hours at the moment.
恐怕我目前不能加班。

(4) I regret that I'm unable to take on extra hours this week.
遗憾我这周不能加班。

9.2.4 If your manager requests you to work beyond regular hours

(1) Regrettably, I won't be available during the weekend, over the holidays, or while I'm on vacation. However, I'll ensure all tasks are up-to-date before I leave.
很遗憾，周末、节假日或休假期间我都没空。但是，我会确保在我离开之前所有的任务都是最新的（没有遗留的待处理或逾期的任务）。

(2) I've ensured everything is up-to-date, and I've provided a list of colleagues you can reach out to if any issues arise while I'm away.
我确保一切都是最新的，同时还提供了一份同事名单，如果我不在的时候有任何问题，您可以联系他们。

(3) If there are critical tasks needing attention outside regular hours, please let me know in advance so I can plan and prioritize effectively.
如果在正常工作时间之外有重要的任务需要处理，请提前告诉我，这样我才能有效地计划和优先处理。

(4) While I'm committed to the project, consistent overtime impacts my work-life balance. Can we discuss a more sustainable schedule or additional support?
虽然我对这个项目很投入，但持续的加班影响了我的工作与生活平衡。我们能讨论一个更可持续的时间表或额外的支持吗？

9.3 Sensitive situations

9.3.1 Asking for a meeting

(1) I'd like to discuss the possibility of a promotion this week. Is there a convenient time for you in the next few days?

我想在这周讨论关于晋升的可能性。接下来的几天里有合适的时间吗？

(2) Could we find a time in the next couple of days to continue our discussion regarding my potential training?
我们能在未来几天找个时间继续讨论我可能接受的培训吗？

(3) Could we set up a brief meeting to chat about a promotion this week?
我们可以在本周安排一个简短的会议来讨论一下晋升的事情吗？

(4) Is now a suitable moment to discuss the company's new structure?
现在是讨论公司新架构的合适时机吗？

9.3.2 Asking for clarification

(1) Can I ask you for some clarification on what you were saying/on the new rules?
我能请您对刚才所说的/新规定做一些澄清吗？

(2) Can you provide more details about the new policy/guidelines?
您能提供更多关于新政策/指导方针的细节吗？

(3) I was a bit confused when you were talking about our new job titles/the new grievance procedure. Could you explain your thinking a bit more?
当您谈到我们的新职位/新的申诉程序时，我有点困惑。您能进一步解释一下您的想法吗？

(4) Could you say a little more about how the merger will affect the department/how we'll be introducing these procedures?
您能进一步说明合并对部门的影响/我们将如何引入这些程序吗？

9.3.3 When you have problems with a colleague

(1) This situation creates challenges for me/the team because it disrupts our workflow, strains communication, and hampers the overall productivity of our projects.
这种情况给我/团队带来了挑战，因为它打乱了我们的工作流程，加大了沟通难度，并且影响了我们项目的总体生产力。

(2) I was assigned to collaborate with Mike, but I've encountered some barriers because our working styles differ significantly.
我被指派与迈克合作，但我遇到了一些障碍，因为我们的工作风格存在很大的差异。

(3) I've made efforts to communicate with Mike, yet the situation remains unchanged.
我已经努力和迈克沟通了，但情况还是没有改变。

(4) I don't know what more I can do now. Would you be able to speak with Julia?
我不知道我现在还能做些什么。您能和茱莉亚谈谈吗？

9.3.4 If your manager asks you about a colleague

(1) Mike is a great colleague to have because he is very precise/always gets back to us in time.
迈克是一个很好的同事，因为他非常认真/总能及时回复我们。

(2) Julia is really good at trouble-shooting/finding new customers.

茱莉亚很擅长解决问题/寻找新客户。

(3) It's not always easy to work with him, especially when we've got a deadline/when there are problems with customers.
和他一起工作并不是那么容易，尤其是当我们要赶工期/与客户产生问题时。

(4) I don't think she's really a team-player/committed to customer care.
我认为她不是一名合格的团队协作者/未能致力于客户服务。

9.4 Methods for dealing with problems when they arise

9.4.1 Problems at work

(1) I'd be grateful if you could review this report/proposal/piece of work for me.
如果您能帮我看一下这份报告/提案/工作，我将不胜感激。

(2) I'm facing some challenges with customer complaints and would value your guidance.
我正面临一些棘手的客户投诉，希望您能给予指导。

(3) Do you have any suggestions for how I can deal with customer complaints?
您对我如何处理顾客投诉有什么建议吗?

(4) I haven't been able to complete the project/achieve our targets for this year, and I would appreciate your advice.
我没能完成这个项目/实现今年的目标，希望您能给予一些建议。

9.4.2 If your manager criticizes you

(1) Thank you for bringing that to my attention.
谢谢您提醒我这件事。

(2) I wasn't aware of that, so thank you for telling me.
我没意识到那一点，谢谢告诉我。

(3) What can I do to put it right?
我该怎么做才能改正呢?

(4) How would you like me to handle it?
您想让我怎么处理?

9.5 Expanding your duties

9.5.1 Asking your manager to agree to something

(1) Would you consider allowing me to work remotely two days a week for better work-life balance?
您能考虑允许我每周远程工作两天以获得更好的工作与生活平衡吗?

(2) I'd like to get involved in the marketing/product launch if that's possible.
如果可能的话，我想参与营销/产品发布。

(3) Would there be an opportunity for me to participate in the public relations activities?
我有机会参加公关活动吗？

(4) I believe I could offer valuable insights in the strategy meetings. Could I have a chance to contribute?
我相信我能在战略会议上提出有价值的见解。我能有机会贡献自己的一份力量吗？

9.5.2 Volunteering ideas

(1) I've spotted a potential method to boost customer loyalty, mind if I share?
我发现了一个提高客户忠诚度的潜在方法，介意我分享一下吗？

(2) I've had an idea to improve our customer loyalty rates/streamline our orders.
我有一个提高顾客忠诚度/简化订单流程的想法。

(3) I've been thinking about our product/market, and I think I've found a way to increase customer retention rates.
我一直在思考我们的产品/市场，我想我找到了一个提高客户保留率的方法。

(4) I have an idea to enhance our product appeal and upsell rate, can we discuss?
我有一个提高我们产品吸引力和提高销售额的想法，可以讨论一下吗？

9.5.3 Taking on new responsibilities/changes in your role

(1) It's been such a great opportunity working on the launch/the sales strategy.
参与产品发布/销售策略的工作是一个很好的机会。

(2) In particular, I've enjoyed doing the public relations and I am quite experienced in getting interviews/getting media coverage.
我特别喜欢做公关工作，而且我在接受采访/获得媒体报道方面非常有经验。

(3) Would it be feasible to retain my current responsibilities?
保留我目前的职责是否可行？

(4) May I inquire about the reasons behind the shift from my current role in product development?
可以问一下把我从目前的产品开发岗调走的原因吗？

9.5.4 Asking to go on a training course/attend an event

(1) I've identified a conference focused on industry innovations. Participation would position us at the forefront of market shifts. Can I pursue it?
我发现了一场专注于行业创新的会议。参会将使我们站在市场变化的前沿。我能参加吗？

(2) I've just heard about a one-day training course on web marketing.
我刚听说有一个为期一天的网络营销培训课程。

(3) I'd be really interested in attending, because I think it would definitely help me with this part of my job.

我很有兴趣参加，因为我认为它肯定会对我的这部分工作有帮助。

(4) I'd be really grateful for the opportunity to go, because it will help me keep up-to-date with industry changes/I'll be learning some useful skills that will help us stay more competitive.
如果能有机会去，我将非常感激，因为这将帮助我跟上行业的最新变化/我将学到一些有用的技能，帮助我们保持更强的竞争力。

9.6 Pay raises and promotions

9.6.1 Asking about your future

(1) I've truly valued my time here. Are there any considerations being made about extending or renewing my contract?
我真的很珍惜在这里的时光。您是否考虑延长或续签我的合同?

(2) Do you know whether my contract will be extended?
您知道我的合同是否会被延长吗?

(3) Have you considered the possibility of my continuation here after my contract ends?
您考虑过我合同结束后继续留在这里的可能性吗?

(4) As my contract approaches its end, I'm eager to discuss potential opportunities for my continued involvement with the team. Any thoughts?
由于我的合同即将到期，我很想讨论一下我继续留在团队的潜在机会。有什么想法吗?

9.6.2 Asking about a pay raise

(1) This year I've optimized our supply chain and implemented cost-saving measures, which have resulted in a 10% increase in profits of $60 million.
今年我优化了我们的供应链，并实施了节约成本的措施，使利润增加了 10%，达到 6000 万美元。

(2) At the beginning of the year, I was set some ambitious sales targets, and as you know, I have consistently exceeded those targets.
年初，我设定了一些雄心勃勃的销售目标，正如您所知，我一直超额完成这些目标。

(3) I'm hoping that my performance/achievements will be rewarded with a pay raise.
我希望我的表现/成就能得到加薪的奖励。

(4) Can you tell me what I would have to do to be considered for a salary increase in the future?
您能告诉我，我要怎么做才有可能在将来得到加薪吗?

9.6.3 Asking about promotion

(1) I'm keen to understand the next steps regarding the promotion we discussed. Has there been any update on this?

我很想知道我们讨论过的晋升的后续步骤。这方面有什么更新吗？

(2) I was wondering if a decision had been made about my promotion.
我想知道关于我的晋升是否已经作出了决定。

(3) Would you know if my promotion is still going ahead/likely to happen?
您知道我的晋升是否在流程中/有可能实现吗？

(4) We discussed a potential promotion two months ago, but I haven't had any formal confirmation yet. Is it still a consideration?
两个月前我们讨论过可能晋升的事，但我还没有得到正式的确认。这还在考虑之中吗？

9.6.4 If you aren't selected for promotion

(1) I respect the decision made and I am eager to understand areas of improvement so I can be a stronger candidate next time.
我尊重您的决定，我渴望了解需要改进的地方，以便下次我可以成为更有竞争力的候选人。

(2) Although I was naturally disappointed that I wasn't selected for the role, I'd love to be considered if another opportunity comes up/arises.
虽然我对没有被选上这个职位很失望，但如果有其他机会的话，我希望被考虑。

(3) While the news was a setback, I'm committed to personal growth and would value any feedback on how I can prepare for future opportunities.
虽然这个消息是一个挫折，但我致力于个人成长，并希望得到任何关于如何为未来的机会做准备的反馈。

(4) I'd appreciate guidance on what steps/skills I should focus on to better align myself with such roles in the future.
我希望能得到指导，告诉我应该关注哪些步骤/技能，以便将来更好地胜任此类职位。

9.7 Resigning and getting fired

9.7.1 What to say when you resign

(1) I asked for this meeting because I want to tell you I've decided to resign.
我要求这次会面是因为我想告诉你们我决定辞职。

(2) This has been a very rewarding job, and it's been a great opportunity to work with you and the team.
这是一份非常有价值的工作，和您及团队一起工作是一个很好的机会。

(3) I've checked in my contract, and I need to give you two weeks' notice. So this means, my last working day will be March 1st.
我查了我的合同，我需要提前两周通知您。也就是说，我最后一个工作日将是 3 月 1 日。

(4) Of course I'll do everything I can to make the hand-over/transition as smooth as possible.
当然，我会尽我所能确保交接/过渡顺利。

9.7.2 Asking for a reference

(1) Given our collaboration and the projects we've worked on, would you be comfortable providing me with a reference?
考虑到我们的合作及我们共同参与的项目，您能给我提供一份推荐信吗？

(2) Would you be able to give me a reference?
您能给我写封推荐信吗？

(3) I value the feedback and guidance you've given me during our time working together. Would it be possible for me to list you as a reference?
我很珍惜我们一起工作期间您给我的反馈和指导。我可以把您列为推荐人吗？

(4) Could I give your name as a future reference?
我可以列出您的名字作为将来的推荐人吗？

9.7.3 If you are fired

(1) While this isn't the outcome I hoped for, I'm grateful for the time spent here and would value any constructive feedback for my future endeavors.
虽然这不是我所希望的结果，但我很感谢在这里度过的时间，并希望今后的工作中能得到一些建设性的反馈意见。

(2) Thank you for your feedback. I'd like to understand more about the decision so I can grow professionally.
谢谢您的反馈。我想更深入地了解这个决定，这样我才能在专业上有所成长。

(3) It's unfortunate it came to this, but I respect the decision and hope to part on good terms.
很遗憾事情发展到这一步，但我尊重这个决定，希望我们能保持良好关系。

(4) Can we discuss the specifics of my transition out, to ensure a smooth handover?
我们能讨论一下我离职的细节，以确保顺利交接吗？

9.7.4 Not saying where you are going

(1) Actually, I haven't got a firm offer yet.
事实上，我还没有收到确定的录用通知。

(2) Well, I intended to take a couple of weeks off before starting a job hunt.
嗯，我打算在开始找工作之前休息几周。

(3) Actually, I'm going to take a bit of a break, and then think about my next move.
事实上，我要休息一段时间，然后再考虑下一步的行动。

(4) Oh, it's just a part-time job for the time being.
哦，这只是一个暂时的兼职工作。

Exercises

9-1 Describe a situation where you had to handle a sensitive situation with your manager. How did you approach it?

9-2 What strategies can you implement to develop trust and respect with your manager?

9-3 Match the phrases in Column A with the appropriate concepts in Column B related to how to talk with your manager.

Column A	Column B
(1) Seeking guidance in handling a team conflict	A. Managing work and deadlines
(2) Discussing your intention to leave the company	B. Pay raises and promotions
(3) Addressing a missed deadline	C. Sensitive situations
(4) Asking for additional responsibilities	D. Expanding your duties
(5) Handling feedback from your supervisor	E. When things going wrong
(6) Reporting an office incident	F. Resigning and getting fired
(7) Requesting a salary increment	G. Developing trust and respect

9-4 Read the four choices marked A, B, C and D, and decide which is the best answer to each question.

(1) When you realize you've made a significant error in a report that's already been sent to the client, you should ____.

A. wait for the client to notice the mistake and bring it up

B. immediately inform your manager and discuss potential solutions

C. hide the mistake and hope nobody notices

D. blame a colleague for not double-checking your work

(2) After receiving a promotion, while your colleague who has been with the company longer than you didn't, the best way to handle the situation is to ____.

A. boast about your promotion in front of your colleague

B. be humble and empathetic, understanding their feelings

C. avoid discussing the promotion with anyone

D. ask your manager to demote you for the sake of team harmony

(3) You want to discuss the possibility of expanding your job role. You should ____.

A. wait until the annual review to bring it up

B. demand additional duties in the next team meeting

C. approach your manager privately and express your interest

D. start doing tasks outside your role without informing anyone

(4) You're not comfortable with a particular assignment due to ethical concerns. The best approach is to ____.

A. resign from the job immediately

B. discuss your concerns with your manager in a constructive manner

C. do the task anyway and ignore your feelings

D. complain to your colleagues about the assignment

(5) You've been considering asking for a pay raise. The most effective approach is to ____.

A. bring it up casually during a lunch break

B. write an anonymous note to HR

C. prepare a list of your contributions and achievements, and request a formal meeting with your manager

D. wait indefinitely until the company decides to increase your salary

(6) When faced with constructive feedback from your manager, you should ____.

A. get defensive and argue against the feedback

B. disregard the feedback since you believe you know better

C. appreciate the feedback and ask for suggestions on improvement

D. request a transfer to a different department

(7) If you're thinking about resigning, the most professional step is to ____.

A. send a resignation text to your manager

B. stop coming to work without notice

C. discuss your intentions with your manager and give appropriate notice

D. share your intention to resign with colleagues before telling your manager

(8) Upon realizing that a colleague is spreading false rumors about you, the most appropriate action is to ____.

A. start a counter-rumor about the colleague

B. confront the colleague aggressively in public

C. discuss the matter privately with the colleague and consider addressing it with your manager if necessary

D. ignore the situation entirely

Unit 10 Communicating with your colleagues

Effective communication with colleagues is crucial for success in the workplace. This unit delves into the significance of teamwork, addressing issues within the office, and the art of being diplomatic. We will also explore ways to engage with challenging colleagues, how to manage when your situation changes, and strategies to deal with four types of problematic peers. Mastering these communication techniques will assist you in collaborating better with others at work and adeptly resolving potential conflicts.

与同事的有效沟通对于职场成功至关重要。本单元将探讨团队合作的重要性，如何应对办公室中的问题及如何灵活变通。我们还会讨论如何与难缠的同事相处，当你的境况发生变化时如何处理，以及面对四种典型有问题的同事的策略。掌握这些沟通技巧，将帮助你在工作中更好地与他人合作，并有效地化解潜在的冲突。

10.1 Team wor

10.1.1 Asking for time to meet

(1) Can we schedule a 15-minute meeting tomorrow morning to talk about the new project/to finalize the arrangements?
我们能在明天上午安排一次 15 分钟的会议，讨论新项目/敲定安排吗？

(2) Can I arrange a meeting with you this afternoon about our project?
我能安排今天下午与你会面讨论我们的项目吗？

(3) I'd appreciate if we could have a brief meeting to align on our next steps. When works best for you?
如果我们能开个碰头会来讨论下一步的工作，我将不胜感激。什么时间最合适？

(4) I'd like to touch base with you regarding our recent developments. Could we set aside some time?
我想与你探讨我们最近的进展。我们能抽出一点时间吗？

10.1.2 Involving colleagues on your projects

(1) We're facing a tight deadline for this. We need to get the proposal out by 10 am on Thursday.
我们的时间很紧。我们需要在星期四上午 10 点前发出提案。

(2) I propose we contact local media first.

我建议我们先联系当地媒体。

(3) I suggest we tackle the problem by first identifying the most frequent complaints.
我建议先找出最常见的投诉来解决问题。

(4) If you're happy with this, I can go ahead.
如果你对此满意，我可以继续。

(5) Could you let me know by the end of today if you've got an alternative idea for solving the problem/getting the work done quicker?
你能在今天结束之前告诉我，你是否有解决问题或更快完成工作的其他办法吗？

(6) If I don't hear back from you by this Friday, I'll assume you're happy for me to go ahead/I'll assume you're fine with this idea.
如果到本周五我还没有收到你的回复，我就认为你同意我这样做/我就认为你同意这个想法。

10.1.3 Asking a colleague for help

(1) Can you give me a hand with the analysis?
你能帮我分析一下吗？

(2) Can I ask you something about your area of expertise?
我能问一些关于你专业领域的问题吗？

(3) Would you have any free time today to help me with the project plan?
你今天有时间帮我做项目计划吗？

(4) Can you take a look at the product launch proposal?
你能看一下产品发布计划书吗？

10.1.4 Refusing someone's help

(1) Thanks, but I'm fine/but it's all under control.
谢谢，但我没事/一切都在控制之中。

(2) Thanks for offering/Thanks for your help, but I think I'm OK.
谢谢你的好意/谢谢你的帮助，但我想我没事。

(3) I think I can manage it, but thanks anyway.
我想我能行，不过还是谢谢你。

(4) Thank you for reaching out. I've got a plan in place, but I'll let you know if anything changes.
谢谢你的帮助。我已经有了一个计划，但如果有什么变化我会告诉你的。

10.1.5 When you can't/don't want to help someone

(1) I'm sorry, but I can't help you at the moment.
对不起，我现在帮不了你。

(2) I'm afraid I can't help you this time.
恐怕这次我帮不了你了。

(3) Let me finish this and then I can help. Are you free after 4 pm today?
我先把手头上的事做完，然后才能帮你。你今天下午 4 点以后有空吗？

(4) That isn't actually my area of expertise.
那实际上不是我的专业领域。

10.1.6 Offering to help a colleague

(1) Would you like a hand with that?
你需要帮忙吗？

(2) Let me know if you need any support on that.
如果你需要任何支持，请告诉我。

(3) Just shout if you'd like me to help with anything.
如果你需要我帮忙，就喊一声。

(4) If there's anything you're not sure about, just ask.
如果有什么不确定的，只管问我。

10.2 Problems in office

10.2.1 Unsafe topics

(1) Sorry, but I really don't want to get involved in this sort of conversation!
对不起，我真的不想参与这种对话！

(2) I don't want to discuss religion/politics at work.
我不想在工作中讨论宗教/政治。

(3) Can we talk about something else?
我们能聊点别的吗？

(4) I'm not comfortable with comments like that.
我对那样的评论感到不舒服。

10.2.2 Not responding to personal questions

(1) Let's focus on another topic, shall we?
我们换个话题吧，好吗？

(2) I'd rather not talk about my personal life at work if you don't mind.
如果你不介意的话，我不想在工作中谈论我的个人生活。

(3) Actually, I'd prefer to keep that sort of thing private.
事实上，我宁愿把这类事情保密。

(4) Do you mind if we don't talk about that? It's a bit too personal for me.
我们不谈那件事你介意吗？这对我来说有点太私人了。

10.2.3 If your colleague talks too much

(1) I've got a meeting shortly, and I need to prepare for it. Can we touch base later?
我马上要参加一个会议，我需要准备一下。我们稍后再沟通好吗？

(2) I'm sorry, but I'm really busy at the moment. I'm afraid I can't chat now.
对不起，我现在真的很忙。恐怕不能聊天。

(3) I'm in the middle of something quite urgent. Mind if we continue this later?
我现在有急事。我们稍后再谈可以吗？

(4) I've got to finish this in the next half hour. Do you mind if we talk later?
我必须在半小时内做完这件事。你介意我们稍后再谈吗？

10.2.4 If your colleague is noisy

(1) I'm sorry, but would you mind keeping the noise down a bit? I can't concentrate/I'm on the phone with a customer.
对不起，你介意小声一点吗？我无法集中精力/我正在和客户通电话。

(2) Would you be okay with using headphones? I find it easier to concentrate in silence.
你可以用耳机吗？我发现安静的时候更容易集中注意力。

(3) I've got an important task to tackle right now. Any chance you could lower the volume?
我现在有一项重要的任务要处理。你能不能把声音关小一点？

(4) I'm trying to review some critical documents right now. It'd be great if you could help keep the noise down.
我现在正在审阅一些重要文件。如果你能帮忙小点声就太好了。

10.2.5 When you don't want to participate in office life

(1) I have other commitments, but I appreciate the invitation.
我有别的事要做，但我很感谢你的邀请。

(2) I'm sorry, but I'd rather not come along to the karaoke/picnic this weekend.
很抱歉，这个周末我不想去卡拉 OK/野餐了。

(3) I hope you don't mind, but I'm not sure I can attend the work party.
我希望你不介意，但我不确定能否参加公司聚会。

(4) I don't think I can make it to the restaurant tonight.
我想我今晚去不了餐厅了。

10.3 Being diplomatic

10.3.1 How to avoid offending your colleague

A colleague may ask you a sensitive question or ask your opinion on something you'd prefer not to

discuss. You can say something like：
同事可能会问你一个敏感的问题，或者问你对一些你不愿意谈论的事情的看法。你可以这样说：

（1） I don't really have an opinion either way.
我对这两种方式都没什么意见。

（2） I'm afraid I wouldn't really know the answer to that.
恐怕我真的不知道那个问题的答案。

（3） I think I'd probably need time to think about that.
我想我可能需要时间来考虑一下。

（4） I'm afraid I can't really discuss this with you now. I need to finish off this paperwork.
恐怕我现在不能和你讨论这个问题。我需要完成这些文书工作。

10. 3. 2 If you and a colleague disagree

（1） Let's find some common ground and work from there.
让我们找到一些共识，然后从那里开始。

（2） I respect your perspective. Can we brainstorm a solution that addresses both our concerns?
我尊重你的观点。我们能头脑风暴出一个解决双方关切问题的方法吗？

（3） What concerns do you have about this idea/proposal/suggestion?
你对这个想法/提议/建议有什么顾虑？

（4） What are you basing your opinion/data on?
你的观点/数据基于什么？

10. 4 Difficult colleagues

10. 4. 1 If a colleague doesn't help you

（1） Would you like me to come back later? I'm free most of the afternoon.
你想让我晚点再来吗？我下午大部分时间都有空。

（2） Is there a better time for me to ask you about this?
有更好的时间让我问你这件事吗？

（3） I know that this is probably an inconvenient time for you, but Mike needs these figures.
我知道现在对你来说可能不方便，但是迈克需要这些数字。

（4） I appreciate you're busy, but this will only take a few minutes.
我知道你很忙，但这只需要几分钟。

10. 4. 2 If a colleague doesn't do his/her share of the work

（1） I don't want to make things difficult for you, but if you don't reply to emails/don't input these data on time, you're slowing down my work too.

我不想为难你，但如果你不回复邮件/不按时输入这些数据，你也拖慢了我的工作。

(2) How can we resolve this situation/problem?
我们该如何解决这个情况/问题?

(3) Actually, this part of the project isn't one of my responsibilities.
事实上，这个项目的这一部分不是我的职责。

(4) I've noticed I'm taking on more tasks related to the project. Could we discuss a more balanced distribution of responsibilities?
我注意到我承担了更多与这个项目相关的任务。我们可以讨论一下更平衡的责任分配吗?

10.4.3 Bypassing your colleague's authority

Sometimes, direct collaboration with a colleague isn't feasible. For instance, if your supervisor assigns you to work with someone from a different department and they're uncooperative, you will have to go back to your supervisor for help.
有时候，与同事直接合作是不可行的。例如，如果你的主管分配你和不同部门的人一起工作，而他们不配合，你就必须回到你的主管那里寻求帮助。

(1) I've asked Julia to get me the product specifications, but I've had no response.
我已经让茱莉亚发我产品规格，但是我没有得到回应。

(2) Could you intervene on my behalf?
你能代表我介入吗?

(3) Could you give me some advice on how to handle it?
你能就如何处理这件事给我一些建议吗?

(4) I've tried collaborating with Mike multiple times, but we're not making any progress. Can you provide some guidance/assistance?
我尝试了很多次与迈克合作，但我们没有取得任何进展。你能提供一些指导/协助吗?

10.4.4 Apologizing to your colleague

If you do something that upsets a colleague or makes his/her job more difficult in some way, apologize.
如果你做了一些让同事不高兴的事情，或者在某种程度上让他/她的工作变得更加困难，请道歉。

(1) I'm so sorry about causing you that delay/getting you the wrong figures.
对于给你带来的延误/给你提供错误的数字，我真的很抱歉。

(2) I hope I didn't cause you too many problems/didn't get you into trouble/delay your work.
我希望没给你造成太多的麻烦/没让你陷入困境/没有延误你的工作。

(3) It was a complete oversight on my part.
这完全是我的疏忽。

(4) I'm really sorry if I offended/upset you in some way. I didn't mean to.
如果我在某些方面冒犯了你/让你不高兴了，我真的很抱歉。我不是故意的。

10.5 A change in your situation

10.5.1 If your role changes

If a change in your role, responsibilities or hours is going to impact your colleagues, you can say something like:

如果你的岗位、职责或工作时间的变化会影响到你的同事，你可以这样说：

(1) As of next week, I won't be handling marketing/I won't be responsible for the warehouse operations.
从下周开始，我将不再负责市场营销/我将不再负责仓库的运营。

(2) I'm going to be handing over the work of stock control to Mike.
我将把库存管理的工作移交给迈克。

(3) I'm going to be working part-time from next month. I'll be in the office on Mondays and Wednesdays.
从下个月开始我将兼职工作。我星期一和星期三都在办公室。

(4) I'm going to be on maternity leave from July 1st. My projects will be handled by Julia during my absence.
我将从 7 月 1 日开始休产假。我不在的时候，我的项目将由茱莉亚负责。

10.5.2 Telling a colleague that you are leaving

(1) I thought it was important to inform you personally: I'll be departing from the company as of July 1st.
我认为有必要亲自通知你：我将于 7 月 1 日离开公司。

(2) I don't know if you've heard, but I've decided to leave the company. I'll be leaving on July 1st.
我不知道你是否听说，我已经决定离开公司。我将在 7 月 1 日离开。

(3) I wanted to let you know that I've handed in my resignation and I'll be leaving on July 1st.
我想让你知道我已经递交了辞职信，将于 7 月 1 日离开。

(4) I wanted you to know that I'll be going on maternity leave from July 1st.
我想告诉你，我将从 7 月 1 日起休产假。

10.5.3 If a colleague asks you if you're leaving

(1) Actually, I'm not job-hunting. I'm happy here/where I am.
事实上，我没有找工作。我在这里很开心/对现在的工作满意。

(2) No, I don't have any plans to leave just yet.
不，我目前还没有离职的计划。

(3) Rumors fly, don't they? I'm content with my position here for now.
谣言满天飞，不是吗？目前我对自己在这里的职位很满意。

(4) I appreciate your concern, but I'm currently committed to my role here.
谢谢你的关心，但我目前在这里尽职尽责。

10. 5. 4 When a colleague is leaving

(1) I'm sorry to hear you're leaving.
听说你要离开，我很难过。
(2) It's been great working with you.
和你一起工作很愉快。
(3) I hope we can stay in touch.
我希望我们能保持联系。
(4) Good luck for the future.
祝你未来好运。

10. 6 Four types of problematic colleagues

Occasionally we have to deal with someone who makes life difficult. Here are some suggestions for what you can say.
有时候我们不得不和一些让生活变得困难的人打交道。以下是一些建议，供你参考。

10. 6. 1 Someone who complains

If someone complains all the time, it can keep you from doing you work, and it also creates a negative atmosphere. Try saying one of these expressions in a neutral tone of voice.
如果有人总是抱怨，这会影响你的工作，也会营造出消极的氛围。试着用一种中性的语气说这些表达。
(1) Mmmm.
嗯。
(2) Oh really?
哦，真的吗？
(3) That's too bad.
那太糟糕了。
(4) Sorry you're having such a bad day.
抱歉你今天这么不顺。
(5) Let's hope the rest of the day gets better.
希望接下来的日子会更好。
(6) Sorry, I can't really talk right now. I've got a deadline to meet/I've got to finish this report.
对不起，我现在真的不能聊。我要赶一个截止日期/我得完成这份报告。

10.6.2 Someone who is uncommunicative

If a colleague doesn't communicate on a professional level, or keeps important details to himself/herself, shared projects can become difficult. Here are some things you can say.
如果同事没有进行专业层面的沟通，或者对重要细节守口如瓶，那么共同的项目就会变得困难。以下是一些你可以说的话。

(1) Mike, to ensure the project goes smoothly, it would be great if we could communicate more openly about any project updates. How does that sound to you?
迈克，为了确保项目顺利进行，如果我们能够更加开放地沟通项目所有进度就太好了。你觉得怎么样？

(2) Mike, could we have regular meetings on the product launch?
迈克，我们可以定期开会讨论产品发布吗？

(3) Julia, it would help our collaboration if we could share updates more frequently. Would that be possible?
茱莉亚，如果我们能更频繁地分享更新，将有助于我们的合作。可以吗？

(4) Julia, I'm concerned that we're missing important details from the product launch. Is there anything you can contribute to the launch?
茱莉亚，我担心我们错过了产品发布的重要细节。你能为发布会贡献什么吗？

10.6.3 Someone who gossips

There's almost always gossip in an office, but it can be damaging to become known as someone who talks too much about others. Say something like:
办公室里几乎总是会有流言蜚语，但如果被人称为多嘴多舌的人，就太糟糕了。你可以这样回应：

(1) I prefer to focus on the task at hand, so let's discuss this later.
我更愿意专注于手头的任务，所以我们以后再讨论这个问题。

(2) Sorry, but I have to go. I've got a lot to do before I can go home.
对不起，我得走了。在回家之前，我有很多事情要做。

(3) I'd better go. I'll catch up with you later.
我得走了。我晚点再找你。

(4) I don't really want to get involved.
我真的不想参与其中。

10.6.4 Someone who takes credit for your ideas

An ambitious but unscrupulous colleague might try to "steal" your idea or to make people believe that an idea was his/hers. You can say this:
一个野心勃勃但不择手段的同事可能会试图"窃取"你的想法，或者让别人相信这个想法是他/她的。你可以这样说：

(1) Actually, I said this very same thing back in the last meeting/my email to you.
实际上，我在上次会议/给你的邮件中也说过同样的话。

(2) Oh, didn't I raise/suggest this point last month?
哦，上个月我不是提出/建议过这个问题吗？

(3) Yes, in fact I suggested this in the last meeting.
是的，实际上我在上次会议提出了这个建议。

(4) I'm so glad you like my idea!
我很高兴你喜欢我的想法！

Exercises

10-1 Describe a situation where being diplomatic would be essential when dealing with a difficult colleague. How would you approach the conversation?

10-2 Name and briefly describe two types of problematic colleagues, and provide one strategy for effectively communicating with each type.

10-3 Match the sentences in Column A with the appropriate concepts in Column B.

Column A	**Column B**
(1) While I understand where you're coming from, I believe another approach might be beneficial.	A. Teamwork
(2) The photocopier has broken down again.	B. A change in your situation
(3) Julia tends to avoid any kind of responsibility.	C. Being diplomatic
(4) I've decided to work remotely starting next month.	D. Difficult colleagues
(5) Let's ensure we divide the tasks evenly among the team.	E. Problems in office
(6) Mike constantly challenges everyone's suggestions in meetings without offering any solutions.	F. Problematic colleagues

10-4 Read the four choices marked A, B, C and D, and decide which is the best answer to each question.

(1) Which of the following is NOT a core aspect of "communicating with your colleagues"? ____.
A. Budgeting B. Teamwork C. Difficult colleagues D. Being diplomatic

(2) How might one best handle a colleague who is reluctant to contribute to team tasks? ____.
A. Ignore the situation
B. Address the situation directly but diplomatically
C. Complain about the colleague to others
D. Overburden them with tasks to force them to contribute

(3) In the context of "communicating with your colleagues", which of the following scenarios best exemplifies the need for being diplomatic? ____.
A. Sharing a clear timetable to distribute team tasks equally
B. Informing the team about a malfunctioning printer
C. Announcing your plans to take a two-week vacation
D. Addressing a colleague's frequent tardiness without assigning blame or causing embarrassment

(4) When faced with problems in the office, the best approach is to ____.
A. blame others
B. keep it to oneself

C. seek solutions collaboratively

D. avoid the office until the problem is resolved

(5) When working with difficult colleagues, an effective strategy is to ____.

A. engage in office gossip

B. be confrontational

C. stay diplomatic and seek mutual understanding

D. avoid them completely

(6) One reason for being diplomatic in communication is to ____.

A. evade responsibility

B. manipulate colleagues

C. foster a positive working environment

D. show superiority

(7) The main reason for communicating a change in your situation to colleagues is to ____.

A. seek sympathy

B. keep them informed and adjust work plans accordingly

C. boast about personal developments

D. create office drama

(8) Teamwork is essential because it ____.

A. allows for longer breaks

B. spreads out responsibility so no one is accountable

C. enhances productivity and fosters creativity

D. ensures one person can dominate

(9) To effectively communicate with colleagues, one must ____.

A. always agree with them

B. always be the loudest in the room

C. understand and respect their viewpoints

D. only interact when necessary

(10) A common challenge in office communication is ____.

A. excessive praise from colleagues

B. frequent vacations

C. dealing with difficult personalities

D. having too few tasks to complete

Unit 11　Communicating with your employees

As a manager, effective communication with your employees is paramount. This unit will guide you on crafting a sound management strategy, aptly delegating tasks, and addressing performance and attitude-related concerns. Additionally, we will delve into how to better hire and support staff, conduct evaluations, and tackle severe performance issues. Understanding and mastering these communication techniques will empower you to cultivate a cohesive and efficient team.
作为一名管理者，与员工的有效沟通是关键。本单元将指导你如何制定管理策略，如何合理地分派任务及处理与绩效和态度相关的问题。我们还会探索如何更好地招聘和支持员工、进行评估，以及应对严重的工作表现问题。深入理解并掌握这些沟通技巧将帮助你建立一个高效、和谐的团队。

11.1　Developing your management strategy

11.1.1　Talking about your communication style/availability

(1) My preferred method of communication is email for non-urgent matters, but feel free to call me directly for immediate concerns.
对于非紧急事项，我首选的沟通方式是发电子邮件，但如果有紧急事项，请直接打电话给我。

(2) I'd prefer to meet weekly for project updates.
我希望每周见一次面，了解项目的最新情况。

(3) I'll only be available in the evening unless it's very urgent/unless there's an emergency.
除非事情非常紧急/有紧急情况，否则我只在晚上有空。

11.1.2　Setting goals and expectations

(1) The most important goal we have this year is to significantly increase our market share.
我们今年最重要的目标是大幅增加市场份额。

(2) In order to achieve these goals/results, we'll need to optimize our operational efficiencies.
为了达到这些目标/结果，我们需要优化我们的运营效率。

(3) I expect/want our customer service team to answer all queries within eight hours.
我希望我们的客服团队能在 8 小时内回答所有问题。

(4) Let me give you an example of what I want you to achieve this year.
让我举个例子来说明我希望你今年完成的目标。

11.2 Delegating tasks

11.2.1 Assigning work

(1) Mike, I want to put you in charge of the new product development team.
迈克，我想让你负责新产品开发团队。

(2) Julia, I'm handing over the sales team training to you.
茱莉亚，我把销售团队的培训交给你。

(3) To complete this project smoothly, you'll need to do three main things. Firstly, coordinate closely with all department heads to ensure resource allocation aligns with project milestones. Secondly, maintain regular communication with stakeholders to keep them updated on progress and gather feedback. Finally, implement rigorous quality checks at each stage to ensure the end product meets our company's standards.
要顺利完成这个项目，你需要做三件主要的事情。首先，与所有部门主管密切协调，确保资源分配与项目里程碑保持一致。其次，与利益相关者保持定期沟通，让他们了解最新的进展并收集反馈。最后，在每个阶段实施严格的质量检查，以确保最终产品符合我们公司的标准。

(4) This project needs to be completed by next Friday. Is that possible?
这个项目需要在下周五之前完成。可行吗？

11.2.2 Managing time and workload

(1) It might be helpful to break down your tasks into urgent versus important. This way, you can tackle the most pressing issues first.
将任务分为紧急任务和重要任务可能会有所帮助。这样，你就可以先处理最紧迫的问题。

(2) If you're often working after 11 am, we need to check your tasks and deadlines.
如果你经常在上午 11 点以后工作，我们需要检查你的任务和截止日期。

(3) If you're feeling overwhelmed, please let me know. We can redistribute tasks or get additional support.
如果你感到不堪重负，请告诉我。我们可以重新分配任务或者提供额外的支持。

(4) If there are tasks that can be delegated to junior team members, let's discuss and assign accordingly.
如果有可以委派给初级团队成员的任务，让我们讨论并相应分配。

11.2.3 Prioritizing

(1) I'd like you to schedule/set aside two days a week to this project.
我希望你每周安排/留出两天来做这个项目。

(2) Please limit the amount of time you spend on social media.
请限制你花在社交媒体上的时间。

(3) Please prioritize marketing over public relations.
请优先考虑营销，而不是公关。

(4) Please make marketing your priority from now on.
从现在开始，请把营销放在首位。

11.3 Managing performance-related issues

11.3.1 Giving feedback

(1) You've settled in really well to the job, and I'm really pleased with your attention to detail/the quality of your work/your efficiency.
你已经很好地适应了这份工作，我对你对细节的关注/你工作的质量/你的效率很满意。

(2) One thing you could consider is asking Mike to give you additional training on customer service/handling customer complaints.
你可以考虑请迈克为你提供客服/处理客户投诉方面的额外培训。

(3) Could you try that from now on/over the next few days?
你能从现在开始/在未来几天试试看吗?

(4) When you call customers, can you introduce yourself right at the beginning?
当你给顾客打电话时，能在开始时做自我介绍吗?

11.3.2 Explain the reasons

(1) Precision and attention to detail in this job are essential to minimize errors and maintain our company's reputation.
在这项工作中，精确度和对细节的关注对于减少错误和维护公司的声誉至关重要。

(2) It's important for someone in this role to sound professional.
对这个职位的人来说，听起来专业是很重要的。

(3) Client satisfaction is a priority for us, so ensuring timely and accurate responses is key.
客户满意度是我们的首要任务，所以确保及时准确的回应是关键。

(4) I need you to use effective communication to perform well in this role.
我需要你运用有效的沟通来做好这个职位。

11.3.3 If a team member is under-performing

(1) The first part of this is fine, but the second part needs more work. In particular, you'll need to check the figures/change the dates. Could you do it again?
第一部分很好，但第二部分需要补充完善。特别是，你需要检查数字/更改日期。你能再做一次吗?

(2) I've noticed that you're running behind on the project.
我注意到你的项目进度落后了。

(3) I've found/noticed a few mistakes in your calculations/your emails to senior management.
我发现/注意到你在计算/给高层管理人员的邮件中有一些错误。

(4) What can you do to reduce the errors?
你能做些什么来减少错误呢?

11.3.4 Dealing with a negative reaction to feedback

(1) I understand that hearing constructive criticism isn't always easy, but my intention is to help you grow and succeed in your role.
我知道听到建设性的批评并不是那么容易，但我的目的是帮助你成长并在你的角色中取得成功。

(2) I realize that it can be difficult to accept this sort of feedback on your work.
我知道要接受对你工作的这种反馈是很困难的。

(3) Feedback is a tool for growth, not an indictment of your abilities or efforts.
反馈是一种使人成长的工具，而不是对你能力或努力的不满。

(4) It's my responsibility to make sure we work well as a team, so I need to give everyone feedback/point out areas for improvement.
确保我们作为一个团队工作顺利是我的责任，所以我需要给每个人反馈/指出需要改进的地方。

11.4 Managing attitude-related issues

11.4.1 Managing conflict

(1) I need to talk to you about what's happening between you and Mike.
我需要跟你谈谈你和迈克之间发生的事。

(2) I expect you and Julia to find a way to resolve these problems.
我希望你和茱莉亚能找到解决这些问题的方法。

(3) It's unacceptable for you to speak like this to Julia.
你这样对茱莉亚说话是不可接受的。

(4) You need to behave in a more professional way with Julia.
你需要以更专业的方式对待茱莉亚。

11.4.2 Dealing with lateness/absence

(1) I've noticed that you're often late in the morning/out of the office.
我注意到你经常早上迟到/不在办公室。

(2) It's come to my attention that you leave work early every day.
我注意到你每天早退。

(3) With this job/role, we need you to start work at 9 am on workdays.
在这个工作/职位上，我们需要你在工作日的早上 9 点开始工作。

(4) It makes other people's work more difficult if you're frequently absent from your desk. Please make sure you're fully available from 9 am to 5 pm.
如果你经常缺勤，别人的工作就会更加困难。请确保你从上午 9 点到下午 5 点都能随时办公。

11.5 Hiring and supporting people

11.5.1 Bringing in new team members

(1) Is there anything you need?
你需要什么吗？

(2) Let me show you around.
我带你转转。

(3) Welcome, Julia! We're really glad to have you join the team.
欢迎你，茱莉亚！我们很高兴你能加入我们的团队。

(4) How are you getting on with your work/the administration?
你的工作/管理进展如何？

11.5.2 Dealing with time off/holidays

(1) If you're thinking of taking an extended holiday, let's discuss so we can plan accordingly.
如果你想延长假期，让我们讨论一下，以便制定相应的计划。

(2) I've noticed that you haven't taken all your holiday entitlement this year. Can you let me know when you want to take it?
我注意到你今年的假期没有休完。你能告诉我你想什么时候休假吗？

(3) Before you finalize your vacation dates, please coordinate with your team to ensure there's coverage during your absence.
在你确定休假日期之前，请和你的团队协调，以确保在你缺席期间有人照看。

(4) We can't carry over your holiday days to next year, so please make sure you use it all up this year.
我们不能把你的假期延续到明年，所以请确保今年用完。

11.5.3 Helping your employee

(1) You don't have to tolerate/put up with abusive language/this harassment.
你不必容忍/忍受侮辱性语言/这种骚扰。

(2) Let me deal with this customer.
让我来接待这位顾客。

(3) If it happens again, let me know and I'll put a stop to it.
如果再发生这种事，告诉我，我会制止的。

(4) Let me know if you need any extra help/resources.
如果你需要任何额外的帮助/资源，请告诉我。

(5) What will you need to fulfill these orders/meet your targets?
你需要什么来完成这些订单/达到你的目标？

(6) Are you OK? /Is everything OK?
你好吗？/一切都好吗？

11.5.4 Thanking your employee

(1) The feedback from our clients about your service has been overwhelmingly positive. Keep up the outstanding work!
客户对你服务的反馈非常积极。再接再厉！

(2) Thank you so much for all your hard work on the site redesign. It went really well because of your effort/involvement/dedication.
非常感谢你为网站重新设计所做的努力。由于你的努力/参与/奉献，一切进展得非常顺利。

(3) Your ability to handle tight deadlines while maintaining the quality of work is commendable. Thank you for staying dedicated.
你能够在时间紧迫的情况下保持工作质量，真的很值得称赞。感谢你保持专注。

(4) You're making excellent progress with our public relations campaign. Great job!
你在我们的公关活动中取得了很好的进展。干得好！

11.6 Evaluations

11.6.1 Giving a performance evaluation

(1) Overall, I've been very happy with your work performance this year.
总的来说，我对你今年的工作表现很满意。

(2) The way you collaborated with the team on the project showed great leadership and problem-solving skills.
你在项目中与团队合作的方式展现了你出色的领导能力和解决问题的能力。

(3) You successfully met all the goals we established last year.
你成功地完成了我们去年设定的所有目标。

(4) Your reports are always detailed and well-structured, making it easier for everyone to understand the data.
你的报告总是内容翔实、结构合理，让每个人都能更容易地理解数据。

11.6.2 Promoting your employee

(1) Have you thought about applying for the team-leader role?
你考虑过申请组长职位吗?

(2) You're in a very good position to apply for the role of team-leader.
你完全有资格申请组长这个职位。

(3) We're really glad that you applied for promotion/the role of team-leader, but we don't think you're ready quite yet.
我们很高兴你申请了晋升/组长一职，但我们认为你还没有准备好。

(4) We'd like you to apply again next year.
我们希望你明年再次申请。

11.7 Serious performance issues

11.7.1 If your employee breaks company rules

(1) We need to be clear on the rules/policy regarding dress codes/confidentiality.
我们需要明确着装要求/保密的规定/政策。

(2) I've noticed that you aren't following company policies regarding personal use of company equipment/harassment and discrimination.
我注意到你没有遵守公司关于个人使用公司设备/骚扰和歧视的政策。

(3) We talked about your absences from work, but you're still taking unscheduled time off.
我们讨论过你缺勤的问题，但你仍然擅自请假。

(4) Unless you change/stop this, you are risking your position here/it will affect your job/I will have to give you an official warning.
除非你改变/停止这样做，否则你会冒失去这个职位的风险/这会影响你的工作/我不得不给你正式警告。

11.7.2 If you have to tell an employee that you are firing him/her

(1) We talked last month about increasing your productivity/changing the way you interact with customers. I'm sorry to say that we haven't seen the improvements we discussed/I'm sorry to say the changes we asked for haven't happened. For this reason, I have to tell you that your

employment here will be terminated on July 1st/with immediate effect (For this reason, we've decided to move you out of the role). I appreciate that this is difficult/that this will put you in a difficult situation. The company can offer you severance pay/a lump sum of $6,000.

上个月我们讨论了如何提高你的工作效率/改变你与客户互动的方式。很抱歉，我们没有看到你做出相应的改进/很抱歉，我们要求的改变没有发生。出于这个原因，我不得不告诉你，你在这里的工作将于7月1日终止/立即终止（出于这个原因，我们决定把你调离这个职位）。我理解这对你来说很困难/这将使你处于一个困难的境地。公司可以给你一笔6000美元的遣散费。

(2) As you recall, during our previous review meeting, we discussed the significance of meeting team objectives and aligning your work with the company's standards. Despite providing additional training and resources, we haven't observed the necessary progress or alignment with our goals. With deep regret, I must inform you that we are ending your employment with the company, effective August 15th. We understand the gravity of this situation and its potential implications on your end. To assist with this transition, the company has decided to offer you a severance package amounting to $6,000. Thank you for your contributions during your tenure here.

你还记得，在上次的总结会上，我们讨论了实现团队目标并使你的工作与公司标准保持一致的重要性。尽管提供了额外的培训和资源，但我们并没有看到必要的进展或与我们目标的一致性。怀着深深的遗憾，我必须通知你，我们将从8月15日起终止你在公司的工作。我们理解这一情况的严重性及对你的潜在影响。为了帮助你顺利过渡，公司决定向你提供6000美元的遣散费。感谢你在任职期间所做的贡献。

11.7.3 In more casual work situations

If your team members work on a more casual or informal basis, it's probably enough just to let them know you won't be offering any more work.

如果你的团队成员工作比较随意或非正式，那么只要让他们知道你不会再提供工作就足够了。

(1) Just a heads up, we won't have more work coming your way. But thank you for your contributions!

提醒一下，我们不会再给你安排更多的工作了。但感谢你的贡献！

(2) Thank you for your work this week, but I won't be needing you next week.

谢谢你本周的工作，但下周我不再需要你了。

(3) We'll be pausing on new tasks for a bit. Thanks for your hard work!

我们将暂停一些新任务。感谢你的辛勤工作！

(4) We're not going to be able to offer you any more work. Thanks anyway.

我们无法为你提供更多的工作。不管怎样，还是谢谢你。

11.7.4 Announcing a redundancy

(1) I genuinely regret to inform you that the company is undergoing a restructuring, and this means we'll be ending some roles, including yours.
我非常遗憾地通知你，公司正在进行重组，这意味着我们将裁掉一些职位，包括你的职位。

(2) I'm sorry to have to tell you that the company cannot extend your contract.
我很遗憾地告诉你，公司不能延长你的合同了。

(3) After much consideration, the company has made the difficult decision not to renew your contract. We truly value the work you've put in.
经过慎重考虑，公司作出了艰难的决定，不再与你续约。我们非常珍视你所付出的努力。

(4) I'm very sorry to tell you that, due to the company's recent financial problems, your position/role will be eliminated.
我很遗憾地告诉你，由于公司最近的财务问题，你的职位/职务将被取消。

11.7.5 When your employee leaves

(1) I'm so sorry you're leaving, but thank you so much for all your hard work.
我很遗憾你要离开，但非常感谢你所有的辛勤工作。

(2) Is there any particular reason why you're leaving?
你要离开有什么特别的原因吗？

(3) It's been a real pleasure to work with you. Good luck in your new job, stay in touch!
很高兴能与你共事。祝你在新工作中好运，保持联系！

(4) I'm sorry to see you go, but congratulations on the new job!
很遗憾你要走了，但恭喜你找到了新工作！

Exercises

11-1 What is the primary advantage of developing a comprehensive management strategy in the workplace?

11-2 Why is it crucial for managers to differentiate between performance-related and attitude-related issues when communicating with employees?

11-3 In the context of "hiring and supporting people", what key aspect should managers prioritize to ensure that employees feel valued and supported?

11-4 Match the phrases in Column A with the appropriate concepts in Column B related to how to talk with your manager.

Column A	Column B
(1) Addressing chronic underperformance	A. Task responsibility
(2) Reviewing an employee's overall contribution	B. Leadership and support

(3) Assigning a task based on an employee's expertise	C. Managing attitude-related issues
(4) The act of entrusting a particular job to an individual	D. Evaluations
(5) Offering guidance and mentorship to subordinates	E. Serious performance issues
(6) Regularly assessing an individual's role and contribution	F. Delegating tasks
(7) Handling issues related to negativity or unprofessional behavior	G. Continuous feedback

11-5 Read the four choices marked A, B, C and D, and decide which is the best answer to each question.

(1) What is the first step in effectively delegating tasks to your employees? ____.

A. Assigning tasks randomly

B. Micromanaging every step

C. Understanding the strengths and weaknesses of each employee

D. Asking for volunteers for every task

(2) How can managers best address serious performance issues? ____.

A. By ignoring them

B. By discussing them in a public setting

C. By having a private, constructive conversation with the concerned employee

D. By instantly terminating the employee

(3) What is a primary objective when hiring and supporting people? ____.

A. To get the cheapest labor possible

B. To find individuals who require minimal training

C. To build a team that contributes positively to the organizational culture

D. To employ as many people as possible

(4) Which of the following is NOT a component of a comprehensive management strategy? ____.

A. Random task assignment

B. Regular evaluations

C. Addressing attitude-related issues

D. Supporting employees' professional growth

(5) When it comes to evaluations, what is crucial for managers to ensure? ____.

A. That they are spontaneous and unpredictable

B. That they highlight only the negatives

C. That they are regular and consistent

D. That they are always comparison-based

(6) Which of the following best describes the approach to managing attitude-related issues? ____.

A. Penalizing immediately

B. Ignoring until it affects performance

C. Addressing through open dialogue and understanding

D. Using peer pressure to change behavior

(7) In terms of performance management, what should managers primarily focus on? ____.

A. The number of hours worked

B. Comparison with other employees

C. Individual growth and achievement against set targets

D. Popularity among team members

Key to exercises

Unit 1 Formal and informal language

1-1 Write a short paragraph explaining a situation where formal language would be appropriate and another where informal language would be better.

Formal language is appropriate in professional settings, such as during a job interview or when writing a business report. In these contexts, it is important to convey respect, clarity, and professionalism, ensuring that the communication is taken seriously and understood by all parties involved. For instance, when presenting quarterly financial results to company executives, using precise and formal language demonstrates competence and attention to detail.

Conversely, informal language is better suited for casual interactions, such as chatting with friends or family or when writing a personal email. This relaxed and conversational tone helps to build rapport and express genuine emotions more naturally. For example, when texting a friend about weekend plans, informal language creates a friendly and approachable atmosphere, making the communication feel more personal and engaging.

1-2 Translate the following Chinglish sentences into standard English.

(1) I can't do it.

(2) This is not my car.

(3) We are just staring at each other.

(4) There are crowds of people everywhere.

(5) You have a very big nose.

(6) Take the medicine.

(7) He can speak English very well.

(8) I really like this movie.

1-3 Read through the two letters below, and identify the differences between them based on formal and informal language.

Formal Letter:

- Greeting: Uses "Dear Sir/Madam", which is a standard formal salutation.
- Introduction: States the purpose of the letter clearly and formally: "I am writing to complain about an incident that occurred in your restaurant at around 7 pm last Friday."
- Details of incident: Describes the incident in a professional manner: "While my

family and I were enjoying our meal, we overheard staff members arguing in the restaurant."

- Impact: Expresses the impact in a composed and respectful tone: "This type of behavior is extremely unprofessional and particularly distressing for my kids to have to hear."
- Relationship: Mentions being a regular customer in a formal way: "My family and I have been regular customers at your restaurant for years, and we hope that we can continue to enjoy your service."
- Action required: Requests action in a polite and formal way: "I trust that you will investigate this matter and take the necessary actions required to ensure customer satisfaction."
- Closure: Ends with a formal closing statement: "I look forward to hearing from you."

Informal Letter:

- Greeting: Uses a casual greeting: "Hello!"
- Introduction: Starts with an informal statement: "Let me tell you what happened when I visited your restaurant last week."
- Details of incident: Describes the incident in a casual and straightforward manner: "I came to the restaurant with my family. The food was on point but then we heard your staff shouting really loudly!"
- Impact: Expresses the impact using informal language and exclamations: "This put me off my food! I mean c'mon is that professional? My child got upset. I was very angry."
- Relationship: Mentions being a regular customer in an informal way: "I'm a regular there."
- Action required: Requests action in a direct and informal way: "You need to look into this matter please. Do what is needed to make sure your customers are happy!"
- Closure: Ends with an informal and urgent closing statement: "Please reply ASAP."

Summary:

- Greeting: Formal uses "Dear Sir/Madam", while informal uses "Hello!"
- Tone: Formal maintains a respectful and composed tone throughout, while informal uses casual and direct language with exclamations.
- Structure: Formal is structured with clear and polite requests, while informal is more conversational and direct.
- Word choice: Formal uses professional language ("distressing" "investigate this matter"), while informal uses everyday language and expressions ("put me off my food" "c'mon").

1-4 Read the four choices marked A, B, C and D, and decide which is the best answer to each question.

(1) B (2) D (3) C (4) C (5) C (6) B (7) B (8) C
(9) A

Unit 2 Email communication

2-1 Below is a sample email. Read it carefully and identify the following parts: salutation, body, closing and signature block.

- Salutation: Dear Team,
- Body: I hope this email finds you well. I'd like to propose a meeting for next Tuesday at 3 pm to discuss our next project. Please let me know if this time works for you.
- Closing: Best regards,
- Signature block:

  Project Manager
  Mike. Turner@ example. com
  +123-456-7890

2-2 Below is an email with formatting errors. Correct the email to ensure proper capitalization, spacing, and empty lines.

> Subject: Update Needed
> Hello Team,
>
> There are some updates in our project. I hope everyone will be available for the meeting on Friday at 2 pm. See you all there.
>
> Thanks,
>
> Mike Turner
> Product Manager
> Mike. Turner@ example. com

2-3 Create your own professional email signature block. Remember to include your full name, position or role, and contact information.

Li Wei
Marketing Manager
Beijing Enterprises Ltd.
1234 Innovation Road, Suite 567
Chaoyang District, Beijing, 100020
Phone: +86 12345678910
Email: li. wei@ beijingenterprises. cn

2-4 Compose a business email based on the following scenario: You are the manager at a tech company and you need to inform your team about a change in the project deadline. Make sure to include all parts of an email and follow proper email etiquette.

Subject: Important: Change in Project Deadline
Dear Team,

I hope this email finds you well.

I am writing to inform you about a change in the project deadline for our current development project. Due to unforeseen circumstances and to ensure the highest quality of our deliverables, the new deadline has been moved to July 15th, 2024.

This extension will provide us with the necessary time to address any remaining issues and to conduct thorough testing to meet our standards of excellence.

Please adjust your schedules accordingly and continue to prioritize your tasks to align with the new timeline. If you encounter any challenges or foresee any potential delays, do not hesitate to reach out to me directly so we can address them promptly.

Thank you for your understanding and cooperation. Let's continue to work together to achieve our project goals.

Best regards,

Li Wei
Marketing Manager
Beijing Enterprises Ltd.
1234 Innovation Road, Suite 567
Chaoyang District, Beijing, 100020
Phone: +86 12345678910
Email: li. wei@ beijingenterprises. cn

Unit 3 How to start a conversation

3-1 Write a brief paragraph discussing why the ability to start a conversation is crucial in a business setting.

The ability to start a conversation is crucial in a business setting because it facilitates effective communication, fosters relationships, and drives collaboration. Initiating conversations can open doors to networking opportunities, enabling professionals to share ideas, seek advice, and establish connections that can lead to business growth and career advancement. It also sets the tone for meetings, encourages open dialogue, and creates an environment where team members feel comfortable expressing their thoughts and concerns. Ultimately, strong conversational skills can enhance teamwork, improve problem-solving, and contribute to a positive workplace culture.

3-2 Using the contexts provided, write a few lines to start a conversation.

(1) Hey, it's been ages! How have you been? I'd love to catch up and hear what you've been up to.

(2) Hi there! How's your day going? I noticed you're reading that book—I've been meaning to check it out. What do you think of it so far?

(3) Nice to meet you! What brings you to this conference? I'm really interested in the keynote about industry trends.

(4) Hi! I couldn't help but notice your laptop sticker. Are you a fan of Star Wars? I'm really into that as well.

3-3 Pair up with a classmate. One of you will choose a context from the list provided and initiate a conversation. The other person will respond. After a few lines of dialogue, switch roles.

(1) A: Hey, I can't believe it's you! It's been so long. How have you been?
B: I know, right? I've been great, just busy with work. How about you?
A: Same here, work has been hectic. It's so nice to see a familiar face here!
B: Absolutely. Let's catch up more after the ceremony!

(2) A: Hi, Sarah! How are you enjoying the event so far?
B: Hey, John! It's been pretty informative. How about you?
A: I'm finding the sessions really insightful. Did you attend the marketing workshop?
B: Yes, I did. It was fantastic. Let's discuss it over coffee later?

(3) A: Hi there, have you been waiting long?
B: Not too long, just about 10 minutes. How about you?
A: Same here. Are you here for the annual check-up too?
B: Yes, I am. I hope it doesn't take much longer!

(4) A: Hi, Mr. Smith! Fancy seeing you here. How's your weekend going?
B: Oh, hi! It's going well, thank you. Just grabbing some coffee. How about yours?
A: Pretty relaxing so far. Enjoying some downtime. Any fun plans for the rest of the weekend?
B: Just catching up on some reading. See you on Monday!

(5) A: Hi, it's a pleasure to meet you. I've heard a lot about your work.
B: Thank you! It's nice to meet you too. What line of work are you in?
A: I'm in product development at TechCorp. I've been following your projects closely.
B: That's great to hear. Let's stay in touch and maybe collaborate in the future.

(6) A: Hey, aren't you in the HR department? I'm in IT. How's your day going?
B: Yes, that's right. My day's going well, thanks. How about yours?
A: Not bad, just fixed a major issue with our servers. Busy day!
B: Sounds hectic! Well, good luck with the rest of your day!

3-4 Match the sentences in Column A with the appropriate situations in Column B related to starting a conversation.

(1) E (2) D (3) A (4) B (5) C

Unit 4 General communication

4-1 Your friend is feeling stressed about an upcoming exam and isn't sure how to prepare. Write a short paragraph offering advice and suggestions on how they might best study and prepare.

Hey [Friend's Name],

I know you're feeling stressed about your upcoming exam, but with the right approach, you can tackle it confidently. Start by creating a study schedule that breaks down the material into manageable chunks, focusing on one topic at a time. Use active study techniques like summarizing notes, teaching the material to someone else, or creating flashcards. Make sure to take regular breaks to avoid burnout and stay refreshed. Also, practice past exam papers to get a feel for the question format and timing. Don't forget to get plenty of rest and eat well, as a healthy body supports a sharp mind. You've got this, and I'm here to help if you need anything!

Best,

[Your Name]

4-2 Read the following situation: A colleague invites you to a party, but you cannot attend because you accidentally double-booked with another event. Write a response to your colleague that includes:

(1) Politely declining the invitation (saying no);

(2) Apologizing for not being able to come;

(3) Responding positively to their news about a promotion they mention in their invitation.

Hi [Colleague's Name],

Thank you so much for inviting me to your party. It sounds like a wonderful event! Unfortunately, I have to decline as I accidentally double-booked with another engagement that evening. I am really sorry for not being able to attend.

Congratulations on your promotion! That's fantastic news and well-deserved. I'm looking forward to catching up with you soon to celebrate your achievement.

Wishing you an amazing time at the party!

Best regards,

[Your Name]

4-3 Match the sentences in Column A with the appropriate situations in Column B related to the general communication.

(1) D (2) B (3) C (4) A

4-4 Read the four choices marked A, B, C and D, and decide which is the best answer to each question.

(1) C (2) C (3) C (4) C

Unit 5 Job interviews

5-1 List five common job interview questions that employers often ask and provide a brief concise answer to each.

- Tell me a little about yourself.
  I have a background in engineering with a focus on project management. I've worked in diverse roles where I've honed my skills in team collaboration and problem-solving, and now I'm looking for new challenges to further develop my career.
- What skills or experiences do you have that would make you successful in this role?
  I have extensive experience in project management and excellent communication skills. My background includes successfully leading teams and delivering projects on time and within budget.
- Where do you see yourself five years from now?
  In five years, I aim to have advanced to a senior management position where I can contribute to strategic decision-making and lead larger projects, while continuing to grow and learn professionally.
- What are your strengths/weaknesses?
  My strengths include strong analytical skills and the ability to work well under pressure. A weakness I'm working on is delegating tasks more effectively to empower my team members.
- Why do you want this job?
  I am passionate about your company's innovative approach and believe that my skills in project management and problem-solving align well with the company's goals. I'm excited about the opportunity to contribute to your team's success.

5-2 Use signposting language to answer the following interview question: Tell me about your previous experience and why you're interested in this role.

First of all, I have five years of experience in project management, where I successfully led multiple projects to completion on time and within budget. For example, in my last role, I managed a team of ten people to deliver a complex project three weeks ahead of schedule. Moreover, I am particularly interested in this role because it offers the opportunity to work with innovative technologies and a dynamic team, which aligns with my career aspirations and personal growth goals.

5-3 Use the STAR method to answer the following interview question: Can you describe a time when you solved a challenging problem at work?

- Situation: At my previous job, we were three days away from a project deadline when we discovered that two of our teams were using incompatible software tools.
- Task: As the project manager, I had to find a solution to ensure the project would be completed on time without any delays.
- Action: I coordinated with both team leaders and devised a plan for one team to convert their work into a compatible format with assistance from staff in other departments.
- Result: Despite the initial setback, we managed to complete the project on time, and the client was extremely satisfied with the outcome.

5-4 Read the following job description and write down five key words or phrases that you could mirror in a job interview.

Team player; Adaptable; Strong background in project management;
Excellent communication skills; Problem-solving attitude

5-5 Pair up with another student. One person will act as the interviewer and the other as the candidate. The interviewer should ask questions based on the key words identified in Exercise 4 and the candidate should respond using the techniques learned in this unit.

Interviewer: Can you tell me about a time when you demonstrated being a team player?

Candidate: Certainly. In my last project, I worked closely with my team to ensure everyone was aligned with our goals. For instance, I facilitated regular team meetings to encourage collaboration and address any issues promptly, which helped us deliver our project successfully.

Interviewer: How do you handle situations that require adaptability?

Candidate: Adaptability is key in any project. For example, when a major client changed their requirements mid-project, I quickly reorganized our team's tasks and priorities, ensuring we met the new expectations without missing our deadline.

Interviewer: Can you describe your experience in project management?

Candidate: I have over five years of experience in project management, leading cross-functional teams to complete projects on time and within budget. My strong organizational skills and ability to foresee and mitigate risks have been crucial in my successful project deliveries.

Interviewer: How do you ensure effective communication within your team?

Candidate: I prioritize clear and open communication by setting up regular check-ins and using collaborative tools to keep everyone informed. For example, I implemented a weekly progress report system that improved transparency and accountability among team members.

Interviewer: Can you give an example of your problem-solving attitude?

Candidate: When faced with a technical issue that threatened to delay our project, I gathered a team of experts to brainstorm and test potential solutions. This proactive approach not only resolved the problem but also enhanced our team's problem-solving capabilities for future projects.

5-6 Read the four choices marked A, B, C and D, and decide which is the best answer to each question.

(1) B (2) C (3) A (4) A (5) A

Unit 6 Presentations

6-1 Introduce yourself informally, and explain your topic in a simple way, with one sentence when making a presentation. Then, introduce yourself formally, and explain your topic in a more detailed way.

Informal Introduction:

Hi everyone! If you don't know me, I'm Mike, and today I'll be talking about our new marketing strategies and how they can benefit us all.

Formal Introduction:

Good morning, everyone. For those who don't know me, my name is Mike, and I work in the marketing department. Today, I'm going to discuss our new marketing strategies in detail, outlining their significance, the implementation process, and the anticipated benefits for our company.

6-2 Which technique would you prefer to use, and why, to introduced your topic and get people's attention from the beginning of your presentation?

I would prefer to use the "Interesting facts or statistics" technique to introduce my topic and get people's attention from the beginning of my presentation. This approach is effective because it immediately engages the audience with surprising or noteworthy information, making them more curious and interested in what I have to say. For example:

Did you know that the average office worker spends eight hours a day at work but only does four hours of productive work? Today, I'm here to talk about time management strategies that can help us double our productive hours and achieve better results.

6-3 Do you have any advice for giving good presentations, in English or any language?

- Know your audience: Research your audience beforehand to tailor your presentation to their interests and needs. This makes your content more relevant and engaging for them.
- Practice thoroughly: Rehearse your presentation multiple times. This helps you become more familiar with the material, reducing anxiety and improving your delivery.
- Use visual aids effectively: Incorporate visuals such as charts, graphs, and images to reinforce your message. Ensure that your slides are not overcrowded with text and that the visuals are clear and relevant.

- Engage with the audience: Maintain eye contact, ask rhetorical questions, and encourage interaction to keep your audience engaged. This helps create a connection and makes your presentation more dynamic.
- Manage your time: Be mindful of the time allocated for your presentation. Ensure that you cover all your points without rushing and leave time for questions at the end.
- Handle questions confidently: Anticipate possible questions and prepare answers. If you don't know an answer, it's okay to acknowledge it and offer to follow up later.
- Use signposting language: Clearly indicate transitions between sections of your presentation. This helps your audience follow along and understand the structure of your talk.
- Stay calm and composed: If you make a mistake or forget something, stay calm. Use filler phrases if needed and keep going. Your composure will reassure the audience and maintain their trust in you.

Unit 7 Chairing a meeting

7-1 Imagine you're chairing a meeting at your company.

(1) Write down three agenda items.

- Review of the quarterly budget.
- Discussion on the new marketing strategy.
- Update on the project milestones.

(2) Practice using different English phrases to introduce each item.

- For the quarterly budget review: First up, we need to discuss our quarterly budget. Let's go over the financial performance and the adjustments needed.
- For the new marketing strategy: Next, let's move on to the discussion about our new marketing strategy. We need to evaluate its potential impact and implementation plan.
- For the project milestones update: Finally, we will update on the project milestones. Mike will lead us through the progress we've made and the challenges we need to address.

7-2 How would you handle distractions during a meeting to ensure the discussion remains on topic? Provide an example scenario and your approach to dealing with it.

Example scenario: During a meeting, one of the attendees starts discussing an unrelated topic about the company's holiday party, causing the discussion to veer off course.

Approach: Let's not get too far off-topic here. I understand the holiday party is important, but we need to focus on today's agenda. We can discuss the party details at the end if time permits. For now, let's get back to discussing our new marketing strategy.

7-3 Match the phrases in Column A with the appropriate concepts in Column B related to chairing a meeting.

(1) E (2) D (3) H (4) I (5) F (6) A (7) G (8) C
(9) B

7-4 Read the four choices marked A, B, C and D, and decide which is the best answer to each question.

(1) C (2) B (3) C (4) B (5) B (6) B (7) B (8) B
(9) B

Unit 8 Negotiation

8-1 Matching negotiation strategies with corresponding statements.

(1) C (2) D (3) E (4) B (5) A

8-2 Read the four choices marked A, B, C and D, and decide which is the best answer to each question.

(1) D (2) D (3) B (4) A (5) C (6) D (7) A (8) C
(9) B (10) A

Unit 9 Communicating with your manager

9-1 Describe a situation where you had to handle a sensitive situation with your manager. How did you approach it?

One sensitive situation I encountered was when I realized I had made a significant error in a report already sent to a client. I approached this situation by immediately informing my manager about the mistake and discussing potential solutions to rectify it. I was honest and took responsibility for the error, and worked with my manager to determine the best course of action to correct the report and communicate the mistake to the client.

9-2 What strategies can you implement to develop trust and respect with your manager? To develop trust and respect with my manager, I can implement the following strategies:

- Make suggestions rather than orders: Using phrases like "Would it be possible to..." instead of direct commands.
- Use hypotheses to make a business case: Presenting ideas with potential outcomes, such as cost reductions or increased efficiency.
- Use polite modal forms: Asking questions like "Could I schedule a meeting?" to show politeness.
- Use past tenses for significant requests: Phrasing important requests in the past tense, like "I was wondering if we could discuss..."
- Be honest: If I don't have information, I will admit it and assure my manager I will find out.
- Being open: Encouraging my manager to share their thoughts and elaborating on their concerns.

9-3 Match the phrases in Column A with the appropriate concepts in Column B related to how to talk with your manager.

(1) E (2) F (3) A (4) D (5) G (6) C (7) B

9-4 Read the four choices marked A, B, C and D, and decide which is the best answer to each question.

(1) B (2) B (3) C (4) B (5) C (6) C (7) C (8) C

Unit 10 Communicating with your colleagues

10-1 Describe a situation where being diplomatic would be essential when dealing with a difficult colleague. How would you approach the conversation?

Situation: Suppose a colleague frequently interrupts during meetings, making it hard for others to express their ideas. This behavior is disrupting the flow of meetings and frustrating the team.

Approach:

- Start by finding a private and neutral setting to have the conversation, ensuring it doesn't feel like a confrontation.
- Use "I" statements to avoid sounding accusatory. For example, "I feel that the team could benefit from hearing everyone's thoughts fully before moving on to the next topic."
- Acknowledge the colleague's enthusiasm and contributions, then gently suggest the need for a more orderly discussion process.
- Propose a constructive solution, such as setting a rule that everyone speaks in turn or using a hand-raising system.
- Ensure the colleague feels heard and valued, emphasizing the goal of improving team dynamics for everyone's benefit.

10-2 Name and briefly describe two types of problematic colleagues, and provide one strategy for effectively communicating with each type.

Type 1: The complainer

Description: This colleague often complains about various aspects of the job, creating a negative atmosphere.

Strategy: Use neutral responses to acknowledge their feelings without engaging in the negativity. For example, saying, "That's too bad" or "Sorry you're having such a bad day" can acknowledge their frustration without encouraging further complaints.

Type 2: The gossip

Description: This colleague frequently engages in and spreads gossip, which can harm team morale and trust.

Strategy: Politely but firmly steer the conversation away from gossip. For instance, you could say, "I prefer to focus on the task at hand, so let's discuss this later," or "I don't really want to get involved."

10-3 Match the sentences in Column A with the appropriate concepts in Column B.

(1) C (2) E (3) F (4) B (5) A (6) D

10-4 Read the four choices marked A, B, C and D, and decide which is the best answer to each question.

(1) A (2) B (3) D (4) C (5) C (6) C (7) B (8) C
(9) C (10) C

Unit 11 Communicating with your employees

11-1 What is the primary advantage of developing a comprehensive management strategy in the workplace?

The primary advantage of developing a comprehensive management strategy is that it helps in crafting a sound management approach, delegating tasks aptly, and addressing performance and attitude-related concerns effectively. This leads to a cohesive and efficient team.

11-2 Why is it crucial for managers to differentiate between performance-related and attitude-related issues when communicating with employees?

It is crucial for managers to differentiate between performance-related and attitude-related issues because each type requires a different approach for resolution. Performance-related issues often need feedback and training, while attitude-related issues might require addressing behavioral changes and managing conflict.

11-3 In the context of "hiring and supporting people", what key aspect should managers prioritize to ensure that employees feel valued and supported?

Managers should prioritize providing adequate support, resources, and feedback to ensure employees feel valued and supported. This includes addressing their needs, offering help, and acknowledging their contributions.

11-4 Match the phrases in Column A with the appropriate concepts in Column B related to how to talk with your manager.

(1) E (2) D (3) A (4) F (5) B (6) G (7) C

11-5 Read the four choices marked A, B, C and D, and decide which is the best answer to each question.

(1) C (2) C (3) C (4) A (5) C (6) C (7) C

